Connect

revised edition

Jack C. Richards
Carlos Barbisan
com Chuck Sandy

Combo 3
Student's book

CAMBRIDGE UNIVERSITY PRESS

CAMBRIDGE
UNIVERSITY PRESS & ASSESSMENT

Shaftesbury Road, Cambridge CB2 8EA, United Kingdom

One Liberty Plaza, 20th Floor, New York, NY 10006, USA

477 Williamstown Road, Port Melbourne, VIC 3207, Australia

314–321, 3rd Floor, Plot 3, Splendor Forum, Jasola District Centre, New Delhi – 110025, India

103 Penang Road, #05-06/07, Visioncrest Commercial, Singapore 238467

Cambridge University Press & Assessment is a department of the University of Cambridge.

We share the University's mission to contribute to society through the pursuit of education, learning and research at the highest international levels of excellence.

www.cambridge.org

© Cambridge University Press & Assessment 2004, 2009, 2015

This publication is in copyright. Subject to statutory exception and to the provisions of relevant collective licensing agreements, no reproduction of any part may take place without the written permission of Cambridge University Press & Assessment.

First published 2004
Second edition 2009
Revised edition 2015

20 19 18 17 16 15 14 13 12 11 10 9

Printed in Brazil by Forma Certa Grafica Digital LTDA

A catalogue record for this publication is available from the British Library

ISBN 978-1-107-54018-7 Combo 3

Additional resources for this publication at www.cambridge.org.br/connectarcade
Cambridge University Press & Assessment has no responsibility for the persistence or accuracy of URLs for external or third-party internet websites referred to in this publication, and does not guarantee that any content on such websites is, or will remain, accurate or appropriate. Information regarding prices, travel timetables, and other factual information given in this work is correct at the time of first printing but Cambridge University Press & Assessment does not guarantee the accuracy of such information thereafter.

Table of Contents

Syllabus iv

Unit 1 Back to School
Lesson 1 New friends 2
Lesson 2 School dinner 4
Mini-review 6
Lesson 3 My new school 8
Lesson 4 After school 10
Get Connected 12
Review 14

Unit 2 Fun Times
Lesson 5 Summer fun 16
Lesson 6 Our trip to Peru 18
Mini-review 20
Lesson 7 School festival 22
Lesson 8 Weekend fun 24
Get Connected 26
Review 28

Unit 3 Going Places
Lesson 9 A homestay 30
Lesson 10 Getting away 32
Mini-review 34
Lesson 11 Explorers 36
Lesson 12 Up and away 38
Get Connected 40
Review 42

Unit 4 Comparisons
Lesson 13 Fun facts 44
Lesson 14 My opinion 46
Mini-review 48
Lesson 15 World trivia 50
Lesson 16 The most 52
Get Connected 54
Review 56

Unit 5 Your Health
Lesson 17 Yoga class 58
Lesson 18 I don't feel well 60
Mini-review 62
Lesson 19 Are you healthy? 64
Lesson 20 Teen health tips 66
Get Connected 68
Review 70

Unit 6 Special Events
Lesson 21 School fund-raiser 72
Lesson 22 A farewell party 74
Mini-review 76
Lesson 23 Dance clothes 78
Lesson 24 After the dance 80
Get Connected 82
Review 84

Unit 7 Our Stories
Lesson 25 The blackout 86
Lesson 26 Scary experiences 88
Mini-review 90
Lesson 27 Close calls 92
Lesson 28 Sharing stories 94
Get Connected 96
Review 98

Unit 8 In the City
Lesson 29 How do I get there? 100
Lesson 30 Street fair 102
Mini-review 104
Lesson 31 Things to do 106
Lesson 32 We didn't go 108
Get Connected 110
Review 112

Games 114

Get Connected Vocabulary Practice 122

Theme Projects 126

Verb List 134

Word List 136

Unit 1
Back to School

Lesson	Function	Grammar	Vocabulary
Lesson 1 New friends	Introducing oneself	Simple present: *Yes / No* questions and short answers; *What, Who,* and *How* questions and answers	Name, age, country origin, habits, likes
Lesson 2 School dinner	Describing what someone is doing; talking about habits	Present continuous and simple present	Common activities
Lesson 3 My new school	Talking about obligations and rules related to school	*have to / don't have to*	Common activities
Lesson 4 After school	Talking about preferences related to after-school clubs	*would like + to* (verb)	After-school clubs
Get Connected	Reading • Listening • Writing		
Theme Project	Make a brochure for a field trip.		

Unit 2
Fun Times

Lesson	Function	Grammar	Vocabulary
Lesson 5 Summer fun	Describing a vacation	Simple past statements: regular verbs	Vacation activities
Lesson 6 Our trip to Peru	Describing a vacation	Simple past statements: irregular verbs	Vacation activities
Lesson 7 School festival	Asking about weekend activities	Simple past *Yes / No* questions	School festivals
Lesson 8 Weekend fun	Talking about weekend activities	Simple past statements: negative	Weekend activities
Get Connected	Reading • Listening • Writing		
Theme Project	Make a group photo album.		

Unit 3
Going Places

Lesson	Function	Grammar	Vocabulary
Lesson 9 A homestay	Talking about feelings	*was / were* statements	Feelings
Lesson 10 Getting away	Talking about past travel experiences	*Was / Were . . . ?*	Popular travel activ and destinations
Lesson 11 Explorers	Asking about school projects	*Wh-* questions with *did*	Research and exploration
Lesson 12 Up and away	Asking about explorers' lives	*Wh-* questions with *was / were* vs. with *did*	Biographical information
Get Connected	Reading • Listening • Writing		
Theme Project	Make a bookmark about an interesting person.		

Unit 4
Comparisons

Lesson	Function	Grammar	Vocabulary
Lesson 13 Fun facts	Making comparisons	Comparative adjectives	Descriptive words
Lesson 14 My opinion	Making comparisons	Comparative adjectives: *more . . . than*	Descriptive words
Lesson 15 World trivia	Describing things with superlatives	Superlative adjectives: *-est*	Descriptive words f animals, places, an cities
Lesson 16 The most	Expressing opinions with superlatives	Superlative adjectives: *the most*	Descriptive words
Get Connected	Reading • Listening • Writing		
Theme Project	Make fact cards.		

Unit 5 Your Health

Lesson	Function	Grammar	Vocabulary
Lesson 17 Yoga class	Describing how to do exercises	Adverbs of manner	Parts of the body
Lesson 18 I don't feel well.	Talking about remedies for illnesses	Clauses with *when*	Common illnesses
Lesson 19 Are you healthy?	Talking about how often someone does healthy activities	*How often . . . ?*	Healthy activities
Lesson 20 Teen health tips	Giving advice about healthy habits	*should / shouldn't*	Advice about healthy activities
Get Connected	Reading • Listening • Writing		
Theme Project	Make a booklet of home remedies for illnesses.		

Unit 6 Special Events

Lesson	Function	Grammar	Vocabulary
Lesson 21 School fund-raiser	Talking about plans for a fund-raiser	*be going to*	Fund-raiser activities
Lesson 22 A farewell party	Talking about party plans	*Wh-* questions with *be going to*	Parties
Lesson 23 Dance clothes	Describing what people are wearing	*Which one / Which ones . . . ?*	Adjectives to describe clothing
Lesson 24 After the dance	Asking who something belongs to	*Whose . . . ?* Possessive pronouns	Party items
Get Connected	Reading • Listening • Writing		
Theme Project	Make a poster of things to put in a time capsule.		

Unit 7 Our Stories

Lesson	Function	Grammar	Vocabulary
Lesson 25 The blackout	Describing experiences	Past continuous statements	Past events and actions
Lesson 26 Scary experiences	Describing experiences	Past continuous + *when*	Past events and actions
Lesson 27 Close calls	Asking about past experiences	Past continuous questions	Past events and actions
Lesson 28 Sharing stories	Sharing opinions about books	Past continuous vs. simple past	Words to describe books
Get Connected	Reading • Listening • Writing		
Theme Project	Finish a story to make a book.		

Unit 8 In the City

Lesson	Function	Grammar	Vocabulary
Lesson 29 How do I get there?	Giving directions to places; describing the location of places	Directions; locations	Locations in a downtown area
Lesson 30 Street fair	Talking about a street fair	*There was a / There were some; There wasn't any / There weren't any; Was there a / Were there any…?*	Items found at a street fair
Lesson 31 Things to do	Making suggestions for activities; expressing preferences about activities	*Why don't we / We could* for suggestions; *I'd rather* for preferences	Popular tourist activities
Lesson 32 We didn't go . . .	Describing the reasons someone did or didn't do something	Clauses with *because*	Tourist activities
Get Connected	Reading • Listening • Writing		
Theme Project	Make a map for an ideal neighborhood.		

Syllabus   v

Lesson 1

New friends

1. Talking about yourself

A Read about these students at Wells International School. Then listen and practice.

T.2

> Hi! My name is Felipe Sanchez. I'm from Chile. I have three brothers and three sisters. I play volleyball. I like salsa music and rock.

> I'm Andrea Soares. I'm from Brazil. I'm 13. I play volleyball and tennis. I like to go shopping, too. I have two brothers and one sister.

> Hello. My name is Luigi Dante, and I'm 14. I'm from Italy. I usually go to bed late, so I don't like to get up in the morning. I get up at 6:30 for school. I like school, but I don't always like to study.

> Hi. I'm Amy Hunt, and this is my brother, Josh. I'm 14 years old. Josh is 13. We're from the U.S. I love soccer and karate. Josh doesn't like sports. He plays video games and listens to music.

> My name's Amanda Stone, but my nickname is Mandy. I'm 14, and I'm from England. In my free time, I hang out with my friends. I also skateboard a lot. I like rock music, too.

B Introduce yourself to the class. Use Part A to help you.

> Hi. My name's Bonny. I'm 14 years old. I have one sister and two brothers. I like soccer and music. I don't like swimming. I take pictures for the school newspaper.

UNIT 1 Back to School

2. Language focus review

Study the chart and complete the questions. Answer them with information from Exercise 1A. Then listen and check.

Simple present			
Yes / No questions and short answers		**What, Who, and How questions and answers**	
Do you **have** any brothers?	**Yes**, I **do**.	**What sport** does she play?	She **plays** soccer.
Does she **play** a sport?	**Yes**, she **does**.	**What time** does he get up?	He **gets** up at 11:00.
Does he **get up** early?	**No**, he **doesn't**.	**Who** has a camera?	**Carl** does.
Do they **like** pizza?	**No**, they **don't**.	**How many** brothers do you have?	I **have** two brothers.
Do you **want to go shopping**?	**Yes**, I **do**.	**How old** is Josh?	He**'s** 13.

1. Q: _Does_ Mandy skateboard? A: _Yes, she does._
2. Q: _____ loves soccer and karate? A: _____
3. Q: _____ brothers does Andrea have? A: _____
4. Q: _____ does Luigi get up? A: _____
5. Q: _____ is Andrea? A: _____
6. Q: _____ Josh like sports? A: _____
7. Q: _____ does Felipe play? A: _____
8. Q: _____ Felipe and Mandy like rock music? A: _____

3. Speaking

A Can you find someone who does these things? Write the questions. Then ask different classmates the questions. Write the names of classmates who answer *Yes, I do*.

Find someone who...	Questions	Classmates who answer *Yes, I do.*
1. plays volleyball	*Do you play volleyball?*	
2. likes rock music		
3. stays up late		
4. has a nickname		
5. has two brothers		

B Ask your classmates about their surveys.

Who plays volleyball?   Jason does.

Lesson 2: School dinner

1. Language focus review

A It's Saturday afternoon before the school dinner. Listen and practice.

Luigi Hey, Amy. It's Luigi. What are you doing?
Amy I'm making a cake.
Luigi Oh, are you making a chocolate cake? I love chocolate cake.
Amy Yes, I am. It's for the school dinner.
Luigi Oh, no! I forgot about the school dinner! I need to make something, too. What can I make?
Amy How about pasta salad? Everyone likes pasta salad.
Luigi Good idea! Thanks, Amy.

B Study the chart. Complete the conversation with the correct forms of the verbs. Then listen and check.

Present continuous		Simple present
Is Amy **making** a cake?	**Yes**, she **is**. / **No**, she **isn't**.	She **makes** great cakes.
What's Amy **doing**?	She**'s talking** to Luigi.	She often **talks** to Luigi.

Note: Nonaction verbs do not usually take the continuous *-ing*.
Examples: *have, know, like, need, want*

Luigi Mom, what are you ___doing___ (do)?
Mom I'm _____ (cook) dinner.
Luigi Are you _____ (make) pasta salad, by any chance?
Mom Yes, I am. Why?
Luigi Well, I _____ (need) some pasta salad for the school dinner tonight.
Mom Oh, that's right – the school dinner! But the *students* always _____ (make) the food for the dinner.
Luigi I know. But I don't _____ (have) time!
Mom OK. You can take this. Does everyone _____ (like) pasta salad?
Luigi Sure. Thanks, Mom!

Unit 1

C Josh is in his room before the school dinner. Look at the photo, and write sentences.

What is he doing now?

(phone) *He's talking on the phone.*   (TV) _____

(pizza) _____   (bed) _____

What else does he do in his free time?

(magazines) *He reads magazines.*   (CDs) _____

(guitar) _____   (trading cards) _____

Is Josh ready for the school dinner?

2. Listening

It's 30 minutes before the school dinner. Some students aren't there yet. What are they doing? Listen and check (✓) the correct sentences.

1. ☐ Joey is riding his bike to school.
   ☐ Joey is walking to school.
2. ☐ Sally is walking the dog.
   ☐ Sally is feeding the dog.
3. ☐ Jake is getting ready.
   ☐ Jake is playing video games.
4. ☐ Buffy is buying drinks.
   ☐ Buffy is buying candy.

3. Speaking

Tell two classmates what you usually do for dinner.

> I usually eat with my family. My mother usually cooks, and we eat at about 7:00. We sit at a table in the kitchen. We talk about school and other things.

Back to School

Lessons 1 & 2 Mini-review

1. Language check

A Complete the questions with *do*, *does*, *what*, *how*, or *who*. Then answer the questions.

1. _Does_ Kendra play basketball?
   (yes) _Yes, she does._
2. _____ Bob and Robin like rap music?
   (yes) _____
3. _____ many sisters does Jorge have?
   (three) _____
4. _____ time _____ Mr. Travis go to work?
   (8:30) _____
5. _____ you want to go to the store?
   (no) _____
6. _____ old is Dana?
   (17) _____
7. _____ Kevin want to play soccer?
   (no) _____
8. _____ has an MP3 player?
   (Tanya) _____

B Look at the picture. Then match the parts of the sentences.

1. Mr. Clark _e_   a. is drinking.
2. Mrs. Clark ____   b. are talking on their phones.
3. Jasmine and Mark ____ c. is talking to Mr. Clark.
4. Miranda ____   d. are playing guitars.
5. The musicians ____   e. is eating.

C Complete Francesca's diary entry with the correct forms of the verbs.

August 29th

Dear Diary,

Today is the first day of school this year, and I'm really excited. I'm ready to go now, but my mom is still ____making____ (make) my lunch. She always _____ (make) great lunches. I really _____ (like) her sandwiches. Right now, my dad is _____ (sit) at the table. He's _____ (read) the newspaper. He usually _____ (go) to work at 7:00, but this morning he's _____ (wait) for me. He _____ (want) to drive me to school today. More later!

2. Listening

A Francesca is at school now. A student interviews her. How will she answer the questions? Listen and check (✓) the correct responses.

1. ☑ Yes, I do.
   ☐ Yes, I am.

2. ☐ No, I don't.
   ☐ I play tennis and soccer.

3. ☐ My father is.
   ☐ My father does.

4. ☐ I don't have any brothers or sisters.
   ☐ No, I don't.

5. ☐ Yes, I am.
   ☐ Yes, I do.

6. ☐ Yes, I do.
   ☐ Yes, I have.

7. ☐ I'm from the United States.
   ☐ I speak English and Spanish.

8. ☐ Yes, I am. I'm Fran.
   ☐ Yes, I do. It's Fran.

B Now listen to the complete interview in Part A. Check your answers.

Time for a Game? See page 114.

Lesson 3: My new school

1. Language focus

A Mandy chats on the Internet with Ken, a friend in England. Listen and practice.

Ken: Hi, Mandy. How's your new school?

Mandy: It's great, but I have to take the bus every morning.

Ken: Well, at least you don't have to take the train anymore!

Mandy: But the bus comes at 6:30 a.m.! I have to get up at 5:45, or I miss it.

Ken: Wow, that's early! What about clothes? Do students have to wear uniforms?

Mandy: No. We don't have to wear uniforms.

Ken: You're lucky! What about lunch?

Mandy: We have to buy lunch in the cafeteria.

Ken: Yuck! Cafeteria food! I hate cafeteria food.

Mandy: Actually, I like school lunch. It's good.

---

have to / don't have to

I **have to** take the bus.
I **don't have to** take the bus.
Do you **have to** take the bus?
  Yes, I do.
  Yes. I **have to** take the bus.
  No, I don't.
  No. I **don't have to** take the bus.
Does Mandy **have to** wear a uniform?
  Yes, she does.
  Yes. She **has to** wear a uniform.
  No, she doesn't.
  No. She **doesn't have to** wear a uniform.

B Write sentences about Mandy. Use *has to* or *doesn't have to*. Then listen and check.

1. (get up at 5:45) *She has to get up at 5:45.*
2. (bus) _____
3. (train) _____
4. (uniform) _____
5. (lunch) _____

C Take turns asking your classmates questions. Ask about the activities in Part B, or use your own ideas.

Do you have to take the bus to school?

Yes, I do.

Do you have to eat in the cafeteria?

No. I don't have to eat in the cafeteria. I usually go home for lunch.

8 Unit 1

2. Word power

A Find two words or phrases that are usually paired with each verb. Then write them next to the verbs.

| ☐ a math class | ✓ at school early | ☐ my classroom | ☐ on time for class | ☐ special gym clothes |
| ☐ an instrument | ☐ a uniform | ☐ my room | ☐ soccer | ☐ the bus |

1. be   *at school early*
2. play
3. wear
4. take
5. clean

B Write three things you have to do and three things you don't have to do. Use words and verb phrases from Part A. Then tell a partner.

I have to . . .

I don't have to . . .

> I have to . . . . . . I don't have to . . . .

3. Listening

A Keiko is an exchange student at Wells International School. Mandy talks to her about her school in Japan. Listen and check (✓) four things she says students have to do there.

- ✓ wear uniforms
- ☐ bring lunch
- ☐ eat in the cafeteria
- ☐ stay in classrooms after lunch
- ☐ clean the school
- ☐ attend school baseball and basketball games
- ☐ go to club activities on weekends

B Look at Part A. Tell a classmate what students have to do and don't have to do at Keiko's school.

> Students have to . . .   They don't have to . . .

Back to School 9

Lesson 4: After school

1. Word power

A Match each verb phrase to its meaning. Then listen and practice.
T.12

1. have fun __e__
2. join a club _____
3. make new friends _____
4. plan activities _____
5. share ideas _____
6. work on class assignments _____

a. meet new people
b. do your homework
c. decide what things to do
d. become a member of a special group
e. have a good time
f. talk about your thoughts with other people

B Read about after-school activities at Wells International School. Then imagine you are a student at the school. Write sentences with the verb phrases.

Chess Club: Chess games for all levels. Have fun and make new friends. Open to students in grades 5–8. Mondays 2:30–3:30

Computer Club: Learn new programs and work on class assignments. Beginners are welcome. Tuesdays 2:30–3:30

Student Council: Become a member of the student council. Share ideas about school life, and plan school activities. Thursdays 2:30–3:30

Drama Club: Perform alone or in groups. Sing, dance, or play an instrument. Mondays and Fridays 2:30–3:30

Volleyball Club: Learn the basic rules of volleyball. Have fun and get some exercise. Join the club today! Tuesdays 2:30–3:30

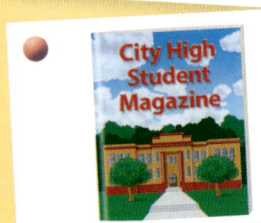

Student Magazine Club: Work with other students on the school magazine. Talk about stories and poems for the magazine. Wednesdays 2:30–3:30

1. have fun _I can have fun in the volleyball club._
2. sing songs _____
3. talk about stories and poems _____
4. work on class assignments _____
5. make new friends _____

10 Unit 1

2. Language focus

A Felipe and Andrea are reading about the after-school activities. Listen and practice.

Felipe Hey, Andrea, look at all these after-school activities!

Andrea Yeah. I'd like to join the volleyball club. I want to exercise and have fun. Would you like to join the club with me?

Felipe Gee, I'd like to, but I can't. I go to the computer club on Tuesdays. How about the drama club? That sounds like fun, and it meets on Mondays. Would you like to join?

Andrea No, I wouldn't! I don't like drama. I like sports. Too bad there isn't a soccer club.

Felipe You can start one! Ask your friends. I'm sure they'd like to join.

Andrea That's a good idea. Would *you* like to join?

Felipe Yes, I would. In fact, I'd like to be the president!

---

would like + to (verb)

I'd like to join the volleyball club.
Would you **like to join** the drama club?
  Yes, I **would**.
  No, I **wouldn't**.

I'd = I would

B Look at the clubs in Exercise 1B. Which club would each student like to join? Write sentences. Then listen and check.

1. **Nick** I want to perform in plays.
   I'd like to join the drama club.

2. **Nina** I like to read and write.
   _____

3. **Rachel** I want to learn how to make a Web site.
   _____

4. **Sam** I want to talk about our school and school life.
   _____

5. **Emily** I want to get some exercise and have fun, too.
   _____

3. Speaking

What clubs in Exercise 1B would you like to join? Ask and answer questions with a classmate.

— Would you like to join the volleyball club?
— No, I wouldn't. I'd like to join the student council.

Back to School 11

UNIT 1 Get Connected

Read

A Read the blog quickly. Are these statements true or false? Write *True* or *False*.

1. The students learn a lot about the waters around San Diego. _____
2. A very big, old boat is one of the classrooms at the Mission Bay Harbor School. _____
3. The students don't learn important life skills. _____

School on the Water

The students at Mission Bay Harbor School in San Diego don't have to sit in a classroom all day. So, what do they do? They spend a lot of time on the **waters** around San Diego studying its history, fish, and **ecology**.

One of their classrooms is the *Sea Flower*, a very large 125-year-old boat. Students learn how to swim, **row** a boat, and even **navigate** a boat up and down a river. And as part of their schoolwork, they have to eat a **crab**!

What other things do students learn? They learn important life skills, like **overcoming fear**. This helps them feel more sure of themselves. Anna Larson, **afraid of** the water before Harbor School, writes in her school journal, "I feel so confident now." She'd like to study marine biology after high school. And another student, Elizabeth Chang, 14, says "I love when we have classes on the *Sea Flower*. It's an incredible boat." So, what do you think? Would you like to go to this school?

More Vocabulary Practice? See page 122.

B 🎧 T.15 Read the blog slowly. Check your answers in Part A.

C Answer the questions.

1. Do the students at the school have to sit in a classroom all day? *No, they don't.*
2. Where do the students spend a lot of time? _____
3. What do the students learn how to do? _____
4. Would Anna Larson like to study marine biology? _____
5. Does Elizabeth Chang like the *Sea Flower*? _____

12 Unit 1

Does he like it?

Listen

A 🎧 T.16 **Nick and Elena talk about school. Listen and answer the questions.**

1. Would Elena like to go to the library with Nick? *Yes, she would.*
2. Who's homeschooled? _____
3. Do Joe's parents teach him everything? _____
4. Does Elena have to take the bus to school and eat cafeteria food? _____
5. Does Nick like school? _____

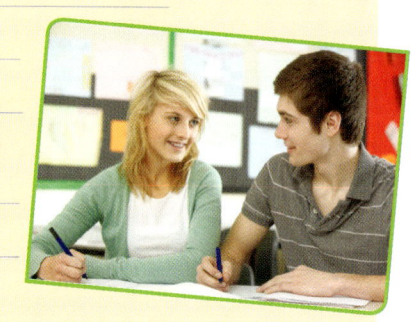

B **What do you think? Write *I agree* or *I disagree*. Give reasons.**

1. It's fun to learn school subjects outside of a classroom. _____
2. Homeschooling is a good idea. _____
3. After-school activities are necessary. _____
4. It's important to have classmates. _____

Your turn

Write

A **Imagine your perfect school. Answer the questions.**

1. Where's the school? (the beach, the mountains, . . .) _____
2. What time do classes start? _____
3. What classes do you have? _____
4. What things do you not have to do? _____
5. What kinds of after-school activities are there? _____
6. What time do you go home? _____

B **Write a paragraph about your perfect school. Use the answers in Part A to help you.**

The school is _____ . Classes start at _____ .
I have _____

Back to School 13

UNIT 1 Review

Language chart review

Simple present	
Yes / No questions	**Short answers**
Do you **like** pizza? **Does** she **swim**?	**Yes**, I **do**. / **No**, I **don't**. **Yes**, she **does**. / **No**, she **doesn't**.

Simple present	
What, Who, How questions	**Answers**
What music does he listen to? **Who** has a computer? **How old** are Sam and Alex?	He **listens** to rock music. Anna **does**. They**'re** 14 years old.

Present continuous vs. simple present	
Present continuous	**Simple present**
Is Joe **talking** on the phone? **Yes**, he **is**. / **No**, he **isn't**. What**'s** Grace **doing**? She**'s reading** a book.	Joe **talks** on the phone a lot. Grace **enjoys** books.

A Read about Peggy and Luiz. Then complete the questions, and write answers.

Peggy	Luiz
14 years old lives in Boston always reads likes hot dogs and pasta	lives in Rio de Janeiro has a computer likes to send e-mail messages always eats hot dogs and pasta

1. Q: _____Does_____ Luiz have a computer?
   A: _Yes, he does._____

2. Q: _____ is Peggy?
   A: _____

3. Q: _____ lives in Rio de Janeiro?
   A: _____

4. Q: _____ Peggy and Luiz like hot dogs?
   A: _____

B Complete the conversations.

1. A ___What's___ Peggy doing?
   B ___She's reading___ a book.
   A She _____ every day!

2. A _____ Luiz eating?
   B _____ hot dogs and pasta.
   A He always _____ hot dogs and pasta.

Language chart review

have to / don't have to
She **has to** go to the library.
She **doesn't have to** go to soccer practice.
Do you **have to** go to the library?
　Yes, I do. / No, I don't. / No. I **don't have to** go to the library.

would like + to (verb)
I'**d like to learn** another language.
Would you **like to learn** French?
　Yes, I would. / No, I wouldn't.

C Look at Sonia and Aldo's schedules. Then write questions and answers.

Sonia's Schedule
5:30 a.m. get up
6:00 a.m. make breakfast
7:00 a.m. take little brother to the park

Aldo's Schedule
11:00 a.m. get up
11:30 a.m. make breakfast
12:30 p.m. clean room

1. **Q:** (Aldo / get up early) _Does Aldo have to get up early?_
   A: _No. He doesn't have to get up early._　OR　_No, he doesn't._

2. **Q:** (Sonia / get up early) _____
   A: _____

3. **Q:** (Aldo and Sonia / make breakfast) _____
   A: _____

D Write conversations.

1. **A** (I / take a trip) _I'd like to take a trip._
   B (Miami) _Would you like to take a trip to Miami?_
   A (Yes) _Yes, I would._

2. **A** (I / join a club) _____
   B (join the chess club) _____
   A (No) _____

3. **A** (I / go to a concert) _____
   B (Smoosh concert) _____
   A (Yes) _____

Take another look!

Circle the correct answer.
Which sentence is closest in meaning to "I'd like to go to the movies after school"?

a. I like to go to the movies after school.
b. I want to go to the movies after school.

Time for the Theme Project?
See page 126.

Lesson 5: Summer fun

1. Language focus

A Jasmine went on a beach vacation. Read her travel blog. Then listen and practice.

T.17

www.jasmine_blog.com

MONDAY, JULY 7

Our first day of vacation in Natal! We (arrived) at our hotel at noon, and we walked to the beach.

My dad rented a dune buggy, and we raced on the sand.

We stopped at a quiet spot, and we stayed there all afternoon.

We snorkeled and played volleyball. What fun!

After dinner, we shopped for souvenirs. We enjoyed looking at all the shops.

Then my sister and I listened to great Brazilian music at a dance club. I danced with some kids from Rio. I even tried a new dance – the forró. It's a lot of fun.

Now it's after midnight, and I have to go to bed. I want to get up early tomorrow. There's so much to do here!

B Study the chart. Then circle 12 more simple past verbs in Part A. Can you find them all?

Simple past statements: regular verbs	

I **walked** to the beach.
Dad **rented** a dune buggy.
My sister and I **tried** a new dance.
You **stayed** there.
We **shopped**.
They **danced** with some kids.
	Note: To spell most simple past verbs, add *-ed*:
	  walk → walked
	For verbs that end in consonant + *y*, change *y* to *i* and add *-ed*:
	  try → tried
	For verbs that end in short vowel + consonant, double the consonant and add *-ed*:
	  shop → shopped

UNIT 2 Fun Times

C Felipe also kept a diary last summer. Complete the sentences from his diary with the correct form of the verbs. Then listen and check.

Monday, July 7   9:30 p.m.
Another vacation day at home. I ____stayed____ (stay) in bed until nine, and then I _____ (walk) to the park. I _____ (practice) volleyball with my friends. Our park volleyball championship game is in September.

In the afternoon, I _____ (listen) to music, and I _____ (clean) my room.

In the evening, I _____ (want) to go out. I _____ (call) Luigi's house, but no one _____ (answer). So I _____ (stay) home and _____ (watch) an old movie on TV. I was so bored. Well, tomorrow is another day.

2. Pronunciation Regular simple past verbs

A Listen. Notice the pronunciation of simple past endings. Then listen again and practice.

/t/	/d/	/ɪd/
stopp**ed** watch**ed**	stay**ed** clean**ed**	visit**ed** wait**ed**

B Listen. Write these verbs in the correct columns.

☐ arrived	☐ called	☐ needed	☐ rented	☐ skated	☐ walked
☑ asked	☐ listened	☐ practiced	☐ shopped	☐ studied	☐ wanted

/t/	/d/	/ɪd/
asked _____	_____ _____	_____ _____
_____ _____	_____ _____	_____ _____

3. Speaking

Work with four classmates. Talk about what you did last summer.

You I visited my cousins, and I played volleyball.
Classmate 1 I stayed home, and I watched a lot of TV.
Classmate 2 I played volleyball, and I cleaned my room a lot.
Classmate 3 I practiced soccer, and I snorkeled.
Classmate 4 I tried in-line skating, and I studied English.

Lesson 6: Our trip to Peru

1. Language focus

A Read about Olivia's trip to Peru last summer. Match the photos to the correct texts. Then listen and check.

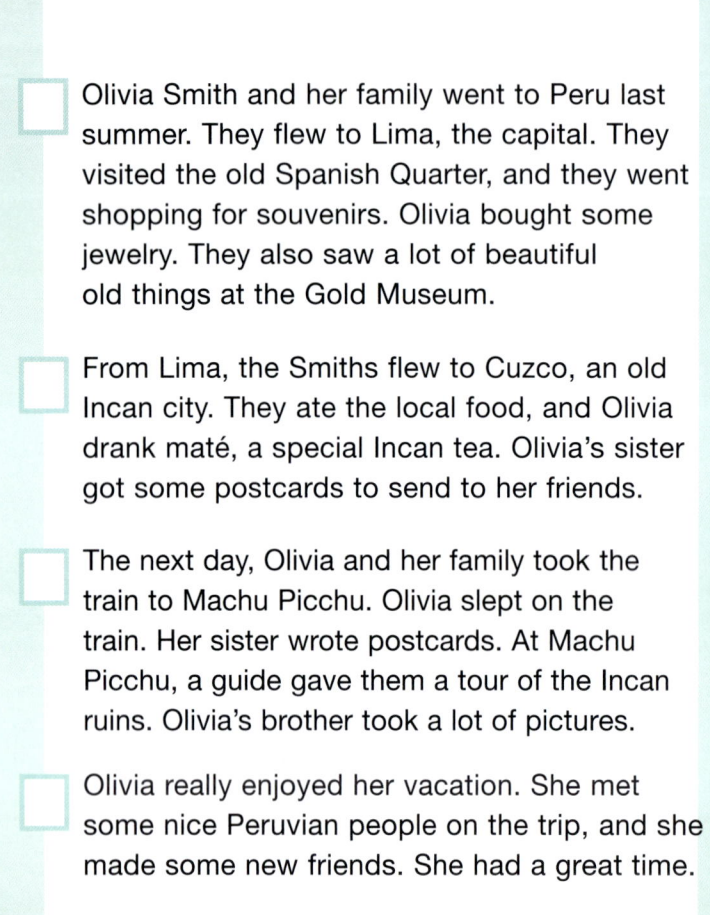

☐ Olivia Smith and her family went to Peru last summer. They flew to Lima, the capital. They visited the old Spanish Quarter, and they went shopping for souvenirs. Olivia bought some jewelry. They also saw a lot of beautiful old things at the Gold Museum.

☐ From Lima, the Smiths flew to Cuzco, an old Incan city. They ate the local food, and Olivia drank maté, a special Incan tea. Olivia's sister got some postcards to send to her friends.

☐ The next day, Olivia and her family took the train to Machu Picchu. Olivia slept on the train. Her sister wrote postcards. At Machu Picchu, a guide gave them a tour of the Incan ruins. Olivia's brother took a lot of pictures.

☐ Olivia really enjoyed her vacation. She met some nice Peruvian people on the trip, and she made some new friends. She had a great time.

B Find the simple past forms of these verbs in Part A. Write them next to the verbs. Then listen and check.

buy	*bought*	have	_____
drink	_____	make	_____
eat	_____	meet	_____
fly	_____	see	_____
get	_____	sleep	_____
give	_____	take	_____
go	_____	write	_____

Simple past statements: irregular verbs

I **had** a great time.
She **drank** maté.
He **took** pictures.
We **went** to Peru last summer.
They **ate** the local food.

C Complete the sentences about the Smiths' trip to Peru. Use the simple past form of the verbs in the box. Then listen and check.

☐ buy ☐ give ☐ have ☐ sleep
☐ fly ☑ go ☐ see ☐ take

1. The Smiths ___went___ to Lima first.
2. Olivia's brother _____ more than 100 pictures.
3. Olivia _____ llamas in Machu Picchu.
4. They _____ fun with their Peruvian friends.
5. Olivia's sister _____ a lot of souvenirs.
6. Their guide _____ them a tour of Cuzco.
7. The Smiths _____ home from Lima.
8. Olivia's parents _____ all the way home.

2. Listening

Olivia talks about her trip to Peru. Listen and check (✓) the things she did there.

1. ☑ danced
   ☐ listened to music
2. ☐ watched soccer
   ☐ played soccer
3. ☐ wrote postcards
   ☐ bought postcards
4. ☐ saw a ring
   ☐ bought a ring
5. ☐ walked
   ☐ rested
6. ☐ slept on the train
   ☐ ate on the train

3. Speaking

A What did you do on your last vacation? Write two true sentences and two false sentences. Use the verbs in Exercise 1B.

True: I had a great time.   False: I slept until 11:00 every day.
1.   1.
2.   2.

B Take turns reading your sentences. Your classmates say *True* or *False*. For false sentences, give the correct information.

You I slept until 11:00 every day.
Classmate True.
You That's false. I got up at 8:00 every morning.

Fun Times 19

Lessons 5 & 6 Mini-review

1. Language check

A Read the messages Martin and Lisa wrote on vacation. Complete each message with the simple past form of the verbs in the box.

- ☑ arrive
- ☐ eat
- ☐ go
- ☐ see
- ☐ sleep
- ☐ take

Hi, Liz!
I'm at the Big Z Ranch in Wyoming. We _arrived_ here yesterday morning. In the afternoon, I _____ cowboys at work on the ranch. For dinner, we _____ outdoors – there was a big barbecue. Last night, we _____ in our own small cabin. Earlier today, we _____ to a rodeo. The cowboys can do some amazing tricks. I _____ a lot of pictures. I'm having a great time! – Martin

- ☐ buy
- ☐ eat
- ☐ have
- ☐ play
- ☐ shop
- ☐ walk

Dear Ben,
I can't believe I'm really in Japan! Yesterday, I _____ a great time. I _____ video games at the Sony Building. Then I _____ for souvenirs for awhile. I _____ some Japanese comic books. I can't read them, but the pictures are cool! I _____ sushi for dinner. Yum! Then we _____ around. I love Tokyo! – Lisa

B Who do you think did the activities below on their vacation, Martin or Lisa? Write sentences.

- ☑ eat in restaurants
- ☐ learn about nature
- ☐ sleep in a sleeping bag
- ☐ go on a hike
- ☐ see tall buildings
- ☐ take a subway

1. _I think Lisa ate in restaurants._
2. _____
3. _____
4. _____
5. _____
6. _____

20 Unit 2

C Look at Valerie's calendar for last week. Then write sentences about her week.

WEEKLY CALENDAR 2016

• Monday	visit Aunt Rita
• Tuesday	go on a hike with Francis
• Wednesday	have a party for Tim
• Thursday	shop at the mall
• Friday	sleep at my grandmother's house
• Saturday	take a dance class
• Sunday	

1. *She visited Aunt Rita on Monday.*
2.
3.
4.
5.
6.

2. Listening

T.25 Josh talks about his trip to Brazil. Listen and number the events in the correct order.

___ visited a mountain
___ bought souvenirs
___ ate lunch with his father's friends
___ saw art
_1_ flew to São Paulo
___ went to a museum
___ wrote e-mails
___ flew to Rio

Time for a Game?
See page 115.

Fun Times

Lesson 7: School festival

1. Word power

A Look at the picture. What can you do at the Jefferson School Festival? Match the activities to the correct verb phrases. Then listen and practice.

☐ buy raffle tickets	☐ go on rides	☐ play games	1 watch the fireworks
☐ eat cotton candy	☐ listen to a band	☐ visit a fun house	☐ win prizes

B Write the verb phrases in Part A in the simple past.

1. *watched the fireworks*
2. _____
3. _____
4. _____
5. _____
6. _____
7. _____
8. _____

22 Unit 2

2. Language focus

A Evan and Sandy talk about their school festival. Listen and practice.

Evan Did you have a good weekend?
Sandy Yes, I did. I had a great weekend.
Evan Did you go anywhere?
Sandy Yes. I went to school on Sunday.
Evan Did you go to a special class?
Sandy No, I didn't. I went to our school festival. I listened to a band and danced, and I ate a lot of cotton candy . . .
Evan Oh, no! I can't believe it! I forgot about the festival. I really wanted to go!
Sandy That's too bad. Did you do anything special on Sunday?
Evan No. I just stayed home all day.

> **Simple past Yes/No questions**
>
> **Did** you **have** a good weekend?
> Yes, I **did**. I **had** a great weekend.
> Yes. I **had** a great weekend.
> **Did** you **go** to a special class?
> No, I **didn't**. I **went** to the school festival.
> No. I **went** to the school festival.

B Luigi and Mandy talk about their school festival. Complete their conversation. Then listen and check.

Luigi Hey, Mandy. ___Did___ you ___go___ to the school festival?
Mandy Yes, I _____ . _____ you go?
Luigi No, I _____ . I had to study.
Mandy That's too bad.
Luigi _____ you _____ a raffle ticket?
Mandy No, I _____ . I never buy raffle tickets. I never win!
Luigi _____ you _____ the fireworks?
Mandy Yes, I _____ . That was the best part!
Luigi Cool! _____ you _____ on any rides?
Mandy Yes, I _____ . I _____ on the bumper cars. I played a lot of games, too.
Luigi Really? _____ you _____ any prizes?
Mandy Yes, I _____ . I won two stuffed animals.
Luigi _____ you _____ to a band?
Mandy Yes, I _____ . I really liked the guitar player.

3. Listening

Amy also went to the festival. What did she do? Listen and check (✓) the things she did.

- ☐ go on rides
- ☐ played games
- ☐ won prizes
- ☐ bought a raffle ticket
- ☐ ate cotton candy
- ☐ ate ice cream
- ☐ danced
- ☐ watched the fireworks

Lesson 8

Weekend fun

1. Language focus

A Amy wrote a blog about her fun weekend. Listen and practice.

> **Simple past statements: negative**
> I **didn't study**.
> Amy **didn't clean** her room.
> They **didn't go** to the party.
>
> didn't = did not

www.amy_blog.com

MY FUN WEEKEND . . .

Friday On Friday night, I played a new video game. I didn't study. I didn't clean my room. I didn't go out of the house. I played my new game all night.

Saturday I didn't want to stay home on Saturday. I left the house at 9 a.m. I went downtown with Jan. We saw a movie and ate pizza at Mario's. Then I went to the school dance. I had a lot of fun. I didn't do any homework.

Sunday On Sunday, I stayed home all day. I didn't go out, but I had fun. I practiced the guitar for the concert next week. I didn't go to Sally's party, but Josh and I made popcorn and listened to music. I didn't check my e-mail, but I called some friends.

B Complete the sentences with the simple past form of the verbs. Use the negative when necessary. Then listen and check.

1. On Friday, Amy ____played____ (play) a video game all night.
2. She ____didn't clean____ (clean) her room on Friday night.
3. On Friday, she _____ (go) out of the house.
4. She _____ (want) to stay home on Saturday.
5. She _____ (go) downtown with Jan.
6. She _____ (do) homework on Saturday.
7. On Sunday, she _____ (go) out.
8. She _____ (have) fun on Sunday.
9. She _____ (listen) to music.
10. She _____ (check) her e-mail.

24 Unit 2

2. Word power

Make verb phrases. Find words or phrases from the box that are usually paired with each verb.

☐ a cake	☐ a lot of homework	☐ a party	☐ some phone calls
☐ dancing	☐ a movie	☐ shopping	☐ to the mall
☑ a great weekend	☐ a new friend	☐ some DVDs	☐ TV

1. have   *a great weekend*
2. go
3. make
4. watch

3. Speaking

A Write four things you did and four things you didn't do last weekend. Use the verb phrases from Exercise 2 or use your own ideas.

Things I did last weekend
1.
2.
3.
4.

Things I didn't do last weekend
1.
2.
3.
4.

B Work with four classmates. Can they guess the four things you did last weekend?

Classmate 1 You watched music videos.
You No. I didn't watch music videos.
Classmate 2 You went shopping.
You Yes. I went shopping.

Fun Times

UNIT 2 Get Connected

Read

A Read the message quickly. Write the names of three animals from the Galapagos Islands.

1. _____ 2. _____ 3. _____

The Amazing Animals of the Galapagos

Dear Lauren,

Hello from the Galapagos Islands. My family and I are here on vacation. We flew here two days ago, and we're taking a ten-day boat trip around the islands.

The **scenery** and the animals here are amazing. We saw **marine iguanas** yesterday. They're cool, and they only live in the Galapagos. And did you know they only eat vegetables? We saw some beautiful birds, too. They had red feet.

What did we do today? This morning we swam and **snorkeled** with some **sea lions**. Later, we photographed some **giant tortoises**. They can weigh up to 551 pounds (250 kilograms). Scientists believe they can live over 100 years. We didn't see any other tortoises like them. They are really nice!

The sad thing is a lot of the animals here are **endangered**. The good thing is many people are working hard now to help save them.

See you soon!
Manuel

More Vocabulary Practice? See page 122.

B 🎧 T.32 Read the message slowly. Check your answers in Part A.

C Are these statements true or false? Write *True* or *False*. Then correct the false statements.

Manuel and his family
1. ~~Lauren~~ went to the Galapagos Islands. *False*
2. They saw marine iguanas and beautiful birds. _____
3. The birds had blue feet. _____
4. They swam and snorkeled with sea lions. _____
5. They photographed some giant sea lions. _____

26   Unit 2

Did you have a good time?

Listen

A Ricardo and Mia talk about vacations. Listen and answer the questions.
T.33

1. Did Ricardo go to Pam's party? *Yes, he did.*
2. Did Mia go to the party, too? _____
3. Did Mia have fun in New York City? _____
4. Did she go to Costa Rica last year? _____
5. Did she eat Japanese food in Costa Rica?
   _____

B What do you think? Answer the questions.

1. Do you think it's good to try the local food?
   _____

2. Do you think it's good to visit museums?
   _____

3. Would you like to hike in a rain forest or visit a big city?
   _____

4. Do you think people with different interests can be good friends?
   _____

Your turn

Write

A Think about your favorite vacation. Answer the questions.

1. Where did you go? _____
2. Where did you stay? _____
3. What did you do? _____
4. What didn't you do? _____
5. What did you see, eat, and buy? _____

B Write an e-mail to your friend about your favorite vacation. Use the answers in Part A to help you.

Hello _____!
I had a great time on my vacation. I went to . . .

Fun Times 27

UNIT 2 Review

Language chart review

Simple past affirmative and negative statements
Regular verbs
I **played** volleyball. I **didn't play** soccer. You **watched** TV. You **didn't watch** a video. He **listened** to jazz. He **didn't listen** to rock.
Irregular verbs
I **went** to the beach. I **didn't go** to the park. You **had** pizza. You **didn't have** a hamburger. She **read** a magazine. She **didn't read** a newspaper.

A Look at the information. Then write sentences in the simple past about Lynn's trip.

Things to do in Washington, D.C.

take a ride in a flight simulator   eat space food
listen to a talk about the solar system   go to the planetarium
see a rock sample from the moon   buy souvenirs

1. *Lynn took a ride in a flight simulator.*
2. _____
3. _____
4. _____
5. _____
6. _____

B Look at Part A again. Correct these false statements about Lynn's trip.

1. Lynn visited New York. *Lynn didn't visit New York. She visited Washington, D.C.*
2. Lynn ate hamburgers. _____
3. Lynn went to the park. _____
4. Lynn listened to music. _____
5. Lynn took a ride in a car. _____
6. Lynn bought movie tickets. _____

Language chart review

Simple past Yes / No questions	
Questions	**Answers**
Did you **go** to the dance?	Yes, I **did**. I **went** with Paul.
	Yes. I **went** to the dance.
Did you **have** fun?	No, I **didn't**. I **didn't have** fun at all.
	No. I **had a terrible time**.

C Look at Parts A and B again. Then write questions and answers.

1. **Molly** Hey, Lynn. Welcome back!
   <u>Did you have a good vacation?</u>
   Lynn Yes, I did. I had a great vacation.

2. **Molly** _____
   Lynn No. I didn't go to California. I went to Washington, D.C.

3. **Molly** _____
   Lynn Yes. I ate space food. It was terrible!

4. **Molly** _____
   Lynn No. I didn't buy movie tickets. I bought souvenirs.

5. **Molly** Did you listen to music?
   Lynn _____

6. **Molly** Did you take a ride in a flight simulator?
   Lynn _____

Take another look!

Circle the correct answer.

1. The simple past forms of regular verbs _____ end in -*ed*.
   a. always   b. sometimes   c. never
2. The simple past forms of irregular verbs _____ end in -*ed*.
   a. always   b. sometimes   c. never

Time for the Theme Project?
See page 127.

Fun Times 29

Lesson 9: A homestay

1. Word power

Beverly and Peter went on a homestay to Puerto Rico. Look at the pictures. Complete the sentences with the words in the box. Then listen and practice.

- ☐ embarrassed
- ☐ exhausted
- ☐ glad
- ☐ relaxed
- ☐ worried
- ☑ excited
- ☐ frustrated
- ☐ homesick
- ☐ surprised

Getting to Puerto Rico

1. She's _excited_.
2. She's _____. 
3. He's _____. 

In Puerto Rico

4. She's _____.
5. He's _____. 
6. She's _____. 

Leaving Puerto Rico

7. He's _____.
8. They're _____. 

Arriving home

9. He's _____.

2. Language focus

A Beverly kept a diary of her trip. Listen and practice.

was / were statements	
I **was** excited.	We **were** glad.
He **was** worried.	We **weren't** homesick.
She **wasn't** worried.	
wasn't = was not	weren't = were not

July 22
Today we flew to Puerto Rico to begin our homestay. I was really excited. My friend, Peter, was worried on the plane, but I wasn't.

July 23
I was very happy to meet my host family. Pablo and Sonia were really friendly, but they spoke very fast. I can't speak Spanish very well, so I was a little frustrated today. Peter's Spanish is excellent, so he wasn't frustrated at all.

August 4
Wow! The two weeks are over. I didn't write in my diary very much. We were really busy every day, so I was too exhausted to write at night.

After the first few days, Peter and I weren't homesick at all. We were glad we came to Puerto Rico. We want to come again next year!

B Read Part A again. Complete the sentences with *was*, *wasn't*, *were*, or *weren't*. Then listen and check.

1. Peter and Beverly _weren't_ on a school trip.
2. Beverly _____ worried on the plane, but Peter _____ .
3. Pablo and Sonia _____ friendly.
4. Peter's Spanish was good, so he _____ frustrated.
5. Beverly and Peter _____ homesick after the first few days.
6. Beverly _____ glad she went to Puerto Rico.

3. Listening

A Other students talk about their homestays. How did they feel? Listen and match their names to their feelings.

1. Howard _d_
2. Maureen ___
3. Mitch ___
4. Tracy ___
5. Wendy ___

a. excited
b. exhausted
c. frustrated
d. homesick
e. surprised

B Work with a classmate. Compare how the students in Part A felt.

> Howard was homesick.

> Tracy wasn't homesick. She was . . .

Going Places 31

Lesson 10: Getting away

1. Word power

A Look at this travel Web site, and match the photos to the correct sentences. Then listen and practice.

TEEN TRAVEL *cool destinations*

www.teentravel75241.dt.br

☐ Dance at a teen club.

☐ Discover New York on a city tour.

☐ Enjoy wild animals on a safari.

☐ Experience the outdoors at a dude ranch.

☐ Go white-water rafting on a river.

1 Have fun at a theme park.

☐ Watch whales from a tour boat.

☐ Spend a week at a ski resort.

B Choose three things from the Web site that you would like to do. Then write sentences.

I'd like to have fun at a theme park.

1. _____
2. _____
3. _____

32 Unit 3

2. Language focus

A Andrea and Felipe are back at school after Thanksgiving break. Listen and practice.

> **Andrea** Hi, Felipe. How was your break? Was it exciting?
> **Felipe** Yeah, very. I went to a dude ranch with my friends.
> **Andrea** Cool! Were you there all week?
> **Felipe** Yes, I was.
> **Andrea** Was it a big ranch?
> **Felipe** No, it wasn't, but I was never bored. We rode horses every day and had campfires every night. What about your break? Was it fun?
> **Andrea** Yes, it was terrific. I went to New York with my family.
> **Felipe** Great! . . . Oh, no! The bell's ringing. We have to go to class. Let's talk more later.

Was / Were . . . ?
Were you there all week? Yes, I was. No, I wasn't. **Was it** a big ranch? Yes, it was. No, it wasn't.

B Andrea and Felipe meet again. Complete their conversation. Then listen and check.

> **Felipe** Hi, again! <u>Was</u> your class interesting?
> **Andrea** It was OK. New York _____ much more fun!
> **Felipe** Yeah. Tell me more about your trip! Was it your first trip to New York?
> **Andrea** Yes, it _____ . We went with Top Tours. We went to the theater and to museums. We shopped a lot, too.
> **Felipe** _____ the weather good?
> **Andrea** No, it _____ . It was a little chilly. And it rained one day. But we had a great time, anyway.
> **Felipe** _____ you in the same hotel all week?
> **Andrea** No, we _____ . We stayed in two different hotels. They were both really nice.

3. Speaking

Imagine you were on one of the trips in Exercise 1A. Tell your classmates how you felt. Can they guess where you were?

> **You** I was very relaxed.
> **Classmate 1** Were you at a dude ranch?
> **You** No, I wasn't.
> **Classmate 2** Were you on a whale-watching tour boat?
> **You** Yes, I was.

Going Places 33

Lessons 9 & 10 Mini-review

1. Language check

A Use the cues to write sentences: ✓ = Yes, ✗ = No

1. George / hungry / last night (✓) *George was hungry last night.*
2. Tonya / frustrated / yesterday (✗) _____
3. Kyle and Millie / excited at the concert (✗) _____
4. Shane and Carl / surprised / at the party (✓) _____
5. You / homesick / in France (✗) _____
6. We / worried / on the bus (✓) _____
7. I / embarrassed / at the dance (✗) _____
8. We / relaxed / on the trip (✓) _____

B Complete the conversation with *was*, *wasn't*, or *were*.

Ned Hi, Lilly. How ___was___ your weekend?

Lilly It _____ exciting. I went to a theme park with my family.

Ned _____ you there all weekend?

Lilly Yes, I _____ .

Ned _____ it a big theme park?

Lilly No, it _____ , but I _____ happy. I love roller coasters! How _____ your weekend?

Ned It _____ OK.

Lilly _____ you at the Big Mountain Ski Resort with your family?

Ned No, I _____ . I _____ at the library. I had to study. We have a big English test today.

Lilly Oh, no! I forgot! Can you help me study at lunch?

Ned Sure. No problem!

C Jeff sent an e-mail to his friend, Pedro. Circle *was* or *were* to complete the sentences.

To: pedrofernadez1456@mr.net
From: jeffmarshall85965@mr.net
Subject: Spring break

Hi, Pedro!

Last week, my classmates and I (was /(were)) on spring break. I went on a white-water rafting trip. It (was / were) fun! I (was / were) on a raft for the first time. I fell out of the raft twice. I (was / were) embarrassed, but later I learned how to stay in the raft.

A lot of my friends went on awesome vacations. Kyle and his dad went camping in the mountains. Kyle likes to camp and hike. He (was / were) very excited about the trip.

Angela took a city tour for three days. She walked and walked. She (was / were) exhausted at the end.

Libby and Gil had fun at a great beach. They (was / were) outside in the sun all day.

On Monday, we (was / were) all sad our break was over. How (was / were) your break? Keep in touch!

Your friend,

Jeff

---

2. Listening

A Read Jeff's e-mail in Exercise 1C again. Then listen to the questions. Check (✓) the correct responses.

1. ☐ Yes, it was.
   ✓ No, it wasn't.

2. ☐ Yes, it was.
   ☐ No, it wasn't.

3. ☐ Yes, they were.
   ☐ No, they weren't.

4. ☐ Yes, he was.
   ☐ No, he wasn't.

5. ☐ Yes, she was.
   ☐ No, she wasn't.

6. ☐ Yes, they were.
   ☐ No, they weren't.

7. ☐ Yes, they were.
   ☐ No, they weren't.

8. ☐ Yes, they were.
   ☐ No, they weren't.

B Now listen to the questions and responses in Part A. Check your answers.

Time for a Game?
See page 116.

Lesson 11: Explorers

1. Language focus

A Luigi tells Josh about a school project. Listen and practice.

Luigi Hey, Josh. I'm exhausted! I stayed up late last night to finish my project.
Josh When did you start it?
Luigi Actually, I started it two weeks ago, but I changed my topic last week.
Josh Why did you do that?
Luigi Well, I started to write about mountain climbing, but I really didn't think it was very interesting.
Josh So, what did you choose for a new topic?
Luigi The *Apollo 11* flight to the moon.
Josh Cool! Where did you get your information?
Luigi I got it at the library. I found some great books and an interesting Web site about Neil Armstrong. He was the first person to walk on the moon.

Wh- questions with *did*
When did you **start**?
I **started** two weeks ago.
Where did you **get** your information?
I **got** it at the library.
Time expressions
this week   a month ago
last week   a year ago
two weeks ago

B Complete the rest of the conversation with the correct words. Then listen and check.

Josh Were you at the library yesterday? I was there, but I didn't see you.
Luigi I was there. When ___did___ (do / did) you leave?
Josh I _____ (leave / left) around 5:00 p.m.
Luigi Oh – I got there at 7:00. How did you _____ (go / went) home?
Josh My mom _____ (drive / drove) me.
Luigi Are you doing a project in your class, too?
Josh Yeah. I just started working on it.
Luigi What did you _____ (choose / chose) for a topic?
Josh I _____ (choose / chose) Shackleton's incredible trip.
Luigi I don't know anything about Shackleton. Where did he _____ (go / went)?
Josh He _____ (go / went) to Antarctica almost 100 years ago.

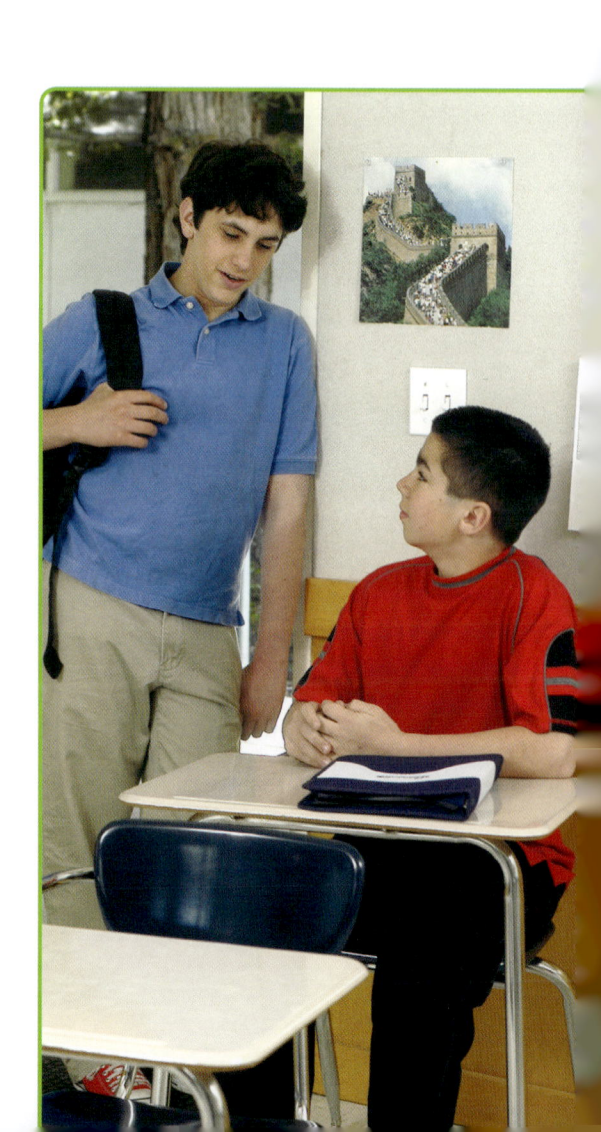

2. Listening

A Two students give their presentations. Listen and number the sentences in the order in which you hear the information.

Christopher Columbus

- [ ] Columbus arrived in North America in 1492.
- [ ] He wanted to find India, but he didn't.
- [ ] Columbus left home at the age of 14 and went to sea.
- [ ] He took four long trips.
- [*1*] He was a very famous explorer.

Lewis and Clark

- [ ] They found new plants and saw a lot of animals.
- [*1*] Lewis and Clark traveled across North America.
- [ ] They made maps.
- [ ] They traveled on foot and by boat.
- [ ] Their trip took two years.

B Luigi's teacher asks questions about the presentations. Listen and check (✓) the correct answers.

1. ☐ He left home and went to school.
   ☑ He left home and went to sea.

2. ☐ He wanted to find India.
   ☐ He wanted to learn to read.

3. ☐ In 1492.
   ☐ For two months.

4. ☐ Two.
   ☐ Four.

5. ☐ From 1804 to 1806.
   ☐ By boat.

6. ☐ They danced.
   ☐ They camped.

3. Speaking

Tell your classmates about a trip or an adventure of your own.
Your classmates ask questions.

You I took a trip with my family.
Classmate 1 Where did you go?
You We went to Colombia.
Classmate 2 When did you go?
You We went two years ago.
Classmate 3 What did you do?
You We visited parks and museums. We snorkeled, too.

Going Places

Lesson 12
Up and away

1. Language focus

A The students had a quiz after their presentations. Listen and practice.

> **Wh- questions with was / were vs. with did**
>
> **Who was** Santos-Dumont?
> He **was** one of the first people to fly.
> **Where did** he grow up?
> He **grew up** in Brazil.
> **When were** his most famous flights?
> His most famous flights **were** in 1901 and 1906.

QUIZ
Alberto Santos-Dumont

1. **Who was Alberto Santos-Dumont?**
   He was one of the first people to fly.
   He built and flew balloons and airplanes.
   In his home country, people call him the father of aviation.

2. **Where did he grow up?**
   He grew up in Brazil. When he was 18 years old, he went to Paris to study.

3. **When did he take his first balloon flight?**
   He took his first balloon flight in 1898.

4. **What was the name of his first balloon?**
   The name of his first balloon was Brazil.

5. **When were his most famous flights?**
   His most famous flights were in 1901 and 1906. In 1901, he flew a balloon around the Eiffel Tower. In 1906, he flew a plane 715 feet in 21 seconds.

6. **What did he do with the prize money from his 1901 flight?**
   He gave half of it to his assistants and half of it to poor people in Brazil.

B Amy is talking to Andrea the day after the quiz. Complete their conversation. Then listen and check.

T.48

Amy Hey, Andrea! We had a quiz yesterday.
Where were (Where were / Where did) you?

Andrea I _____ (was / did) at home.
I didn't feel well.

Amy Oh, that's too bad. Are you OK now?

Andrea Yeah. _____ (How was / How did) the quiz?

Amy It _____ (wasn't / didn't) too difficult. Do you have to take it today?

Andrea I think so. And I didn't study much, so I'm worried.

Amy Why didn't you study? _____ (What were / What did) you do all day?

Andrea I _____ (sleep / slept)!

C Complete the quiz questions about Lewis and Clark with *Wh-* question words and *was*, *were*, or *did*. Then listen and check.

T.49

1. **Q:** _Who were_ Lewis and Clark? **A:** They were American explorers.
2. **Q:** _____ they start their exploration? **A:** They started their exploration in May 1804.
3. **Q:** _____ they find? **A:** They found new plants and animals.
4. **Q:** _____ they meet? **A:** They met many Native American people.
5. **Q:** _____ their guide? **A:** Their guide was Sacagawea, a Native American woman.

2. Speaking

A Think of a school project or a report you did about a famous person in history. Write answers to the questions.

1. Who was your project about? _____
2. Where did he or she live? _____
3. What did he or she do? _____
4. Where did you get your information? _____
5. Who were your listeners or readers? _____

B Ask and answer the questions in Part A with a classmate.

Who was your project about?   It was about Henry Ford.

Going Places 39

UNIT 3 Get Connected

Read

A Read the article quickly. Check (✓) the false statement.

☐ 1. Joshua explores places by airplane.

☐ 2. Joshua learns skills from the local people but travels alone.

☐ 3. Joshua's Siberia to Alaska adventure was one of his favorites.

Joshua Harley, A Modern Day Explorer

Joshua Harley was born in Canada in 1958. His father was a **diplomat**, and Joshua dreamed of traveling around the world like his dad. His dream came true – Joshua became an explorer. But he doesn't travel the world in an airplane. He finds a place he wants to explore, and then he lives with the local people. He learns important skills from them, and then uses those **skills** to explore the place he's visiting. He doesn't use **modern** things like GPS or computers, and he likes to travel alone.

Joshua's explorations are often dangerous, but he likes them. One of his favorite adventures was in 2010. He wanted to travel alone across the ice from Siberia to Alaska. So, he went to Siberia and lived with the people there. He learned how to drive a dog team and live like the people. He traveled 500 **miles** (800 kilometers) with only a dog team. The weather was really bad. There was a lot of snow, wind, and ice, so the **journey** was very difficult. Joshua almost lost the dog team, and he almost died, so he **ended** his journey early. It was **scary**, but he says he learned a lot.

More Vocabulary Practice? See page 123

B 🎧 T.50 Read the article slowly. Check your answer in Part A.

C Answer the questions.

1. Where was Joshua Harley born?
   He was born in Canada.

2. Was Joshua's father a doctor?
   _____

3. Where did Joshua go in 2010?
   _____

4. What did he learn how to do?
   _____

5. How was the weather on Joshua's journey in Siberia?
   _____

It was really an adventure!

Listen

A 🎧 T.51 **Laurie and Will talk about an adventure. Listen and answer the questions.**

1. Who did Laurie go mountain climbing with?
   She went mountain climbing with her uncle.
2. When did Laurie go mountain climbing? _____
3. Was Laurie scared? _____
4. Where did Laurie and her uncle stay? _____
5. Was Laurie sad to see the other climbers? _____

B **What do you think? Write *I agree* or *I disagree*. Give reasons.**

1. All adventures are dangerous. _____
2. It's good to have an adventure on vacation. _____
3. Mountain climbing is a dangerous sport. _____
4. Cell phones can always help people. _____

Your turn

Write

A **Imagine you were just on an amazing adventure. Answer the questions about your adventure.**

1. Where did you go? _____
2. When did you go? _____
3. Who did you go with? _____
4. What did you take with you? _____
5. What happened on your adventure? _____
6. Were you excited to get home? Why or why not? _____

B **Write a paragraph about your adventure. Use the answers in Part A to help you.**

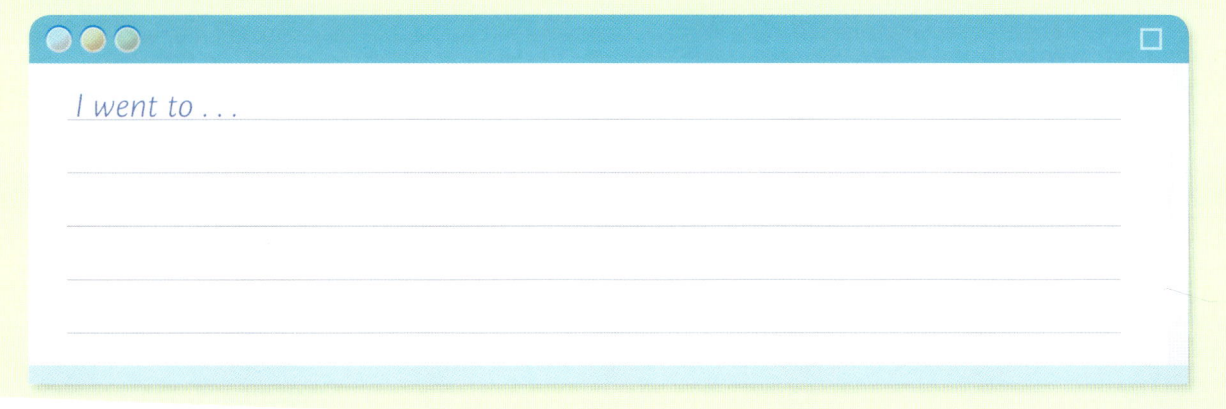

I went to . . .

Going Places 41

UNIT 3 Review

Language chart review

was / were statements

I **was** home. I **wasn't** at the party.
He **was** excited. He **wasn't** worried.
They **were** friendly. They **weren't** shy.

Wh- questions with did

When did you **get** here?   **What time did** you **go** to bed?
I **got** here two days ago.   I **went** to bed at 11:00.

A Write *Wh-* questions with *did*, and complete the answers.
Use the words in the box. Pay attention to the underlined words.

☐ get home / exhausted ☐ go / homesick ☐ spill / embarrassed
☐ go / glad ☑ meet / excited ☐ talk to / bored

1. **A** *Who did you meet?*
   B I met <u>my favorite basketball player</u>.
   I was excited.

2. **A** _____
   B I spilled <u>my juice</u> all over the table.
   _____

3. **A** _____
   B I got home at <u>2:00 a.m.</u>!
   _____

4. **A** _____
   B I went to the beach <u>yesterday</u>. It was a beautiful day.
   _____

5. **A** _____
   B I didn't talk to <u>anyone</u> last night.
   _____

6. **A** _____
   B We went to <u>camp</u>. We missed our families.

42 Unit 3

Language chart review

Was / Were ... ?
Were you in class last Monday?
Yes, I was. / No, I wasn't.
Was it fun?
Yes, it was. / No, it wasn't.

Wh- questions with was / were
Where were you born?
 I was born in San Juan.
When was your first concert?
 It was in 2015.
What was his name?
 His name was George Harrison.
Who was the drummer for the Beatles?
 Ringo Starr was the drummer.

B Read the answers. Then write questions about the underlined words.

1. **Q:** *What was the Model T Ford?*
   A: The Model T Ford was <u>a car</u>.
   Q: _____
   A: The first Model T Ford was <u>black</u>.
   Q: _____
   A: No, it wasn't. The first Model T Ford wasn't <u>fast</u>.

2. **Q:** _____
   A: The Beatles were <u>a British musical group</u>.
   Q: _____
   A: They played <u>rock music</u>.
   Q: _____
   A: They came to the U.S. <u>in 1964</u>.

C Look at Part B again. Use the information to write questions and short answers.

1. (the Model T Ford / an airplane)
   Q: *Was the Model T Ford an airplane?*   **A:** *No, it wasn't.*
2. (the first Model T Ford / slow)
   Q: _____   **A:** _____
3. (The Beatles / a hip-hop group)
   Q: _____   **A:** _____
4. (The Beatles / in the U.S. in 1964)
   Q: _____   **A:** _____

Take another look!

Circle the correct answer.

We _____ use *did* in questions with *was / were*.
a. always   b. sometimes   c. never

Time for the Theme Project? See page 128.

Going Places 43

Lesson 13: Fun facts

1. Language focus

A Andrea and Mandy are playing Fun Facts. Felipe joins them. Listen and practice.

T.52

Felipe Hey! What are you guys doing?
Andrea We're playing Fun Facts. Come and join us.
Mandy OK, Andrea. It's your turn. The moon is bigger than the sun. True or false?
Andrea That's easy. It's false. The moon is smaller than the sun.
Mandy Right. That's five points for you.
Andrea This one's for you, Felipe. Which is warmer, the North Pole or the South Pole?
Felipe I think the South Pole is warmer.
Andrea No, sorry. That's wrong. The North Pole is warmer than the South Pole.

B Study the chart. Write the comparative forms of the adjectives.

Comparative adjectives	
For regular one-syllable adjectives: small → smal**ler** warm → warm**er**	For adjectives ending in *y*: easy → eas**ier** busy → bus**ier**
For adjectives ending in consonant + vowel + consonant: big → big**ger** hot → hot**ter**	Comparative adjectives are followed by *than*. The moon is **smaller than** the sun.

1. warm   *warmer*
2. hot
3. easy
4. slow
5. cold
6. tall
7. hard
8. fast
9. short
10. big
11. busy
12. long

C Complete the sentences with your own ideas. Then tell a classmate.

1. _____ is warmer than _____ .
2. _____ is easier than _____ .
3. _____ is slower than _____ .
4. _____ is bigger than _____ .
5. _____ is longer than _____ .

Miami is warmer than Chicag

UNIT 4 Comparisons

D Write two sentences about the sets of photos. Use the pairs of words in the box. Then listen and check.

☐ big – small   ☐ fast – slow   ☐ cold – hot   ☑ long – short

1 the Amazon River / the Mississippi River

2 speedboats / canoes

3 basketballs / golf balls

4 the Alps / the Sahara

1. *The Amazon River is longer than the Mississippi River.*
   The Mississippi River is shorter than the Amazon River.

2.

3.

4.

2. Listening

Kelly is a very curious little girl. She asks her father a lot of questions. Listen to their conversation. Then circle the correct words.

1. Germany is (**larger** / smaller) than England.
2. Bears are (faster / slower) than lions.
3. The Euphrates River is (longer / shorter) than the Nile River.
4. Water is (lighter / heavier) than snow.
5. Miami is (warmer / cooler) than Quito.

Comparisons 45

Lesson 14: My opinion

1. Language focus

A Read the survey. Listen and practice. Then check (✓) your opinions.

> **Comparative adjectives:** *more ... than*
>
> Use *more ... than* with adjectives of two or more syllables:
> *popular* → *more popular*
> Soccer is **more popular than** volleyball.
>
> *interesting* → *more interesting*
> Books are **more interesting than** video games.

TEEN OPINION SURVEY

Do you agree or disagree? | I agree. | I disagree.

1. Soccer is more popular than volleyball.
2. Books are more interesting than video games.
3. Roller coasters are more exciting than bumper cars.
4. Math is more useful than history.
5. Saturdays are more relaxing than Sundays.
6. Movies are more entertaining than TV shows.
7. Pizza is more delicious than spaghetti.
8. Surfing is more challenging than tennis.
9. Elephants are more dangerous than lions.
10. Science is more important than history.

B Compare your opinions from Part A with a classmate.

> I think soccer is more popular than volleyball.

> I disagree. I think volleyball is more popular than soccer.

46 Unit 4

C What do you think? Compare these things. Use the words in the box or your own ideas.

☐ dangerous ☐ delicious ☐ entertaining ☐ important ☑ popular

1. (T-shirts / sweaters)
   T-shirts are more popular than sweaters.

2. (chocolate ice cream / strawberry ice cream)

3. (books / newspapers)

4. (karate / hockey)

5. (rap music / country music)

2. Speaking

What's your opinion? Compare these things using the words in the box or your own ideas. Then tell a classmate.

☐ difficult ☐ exciting ☐ important ☐ popular ☐ relaxing ☐ useful

I think paper books are more popular than e-books.

Really? I think e-books are more popular than paper books.

Lessons 13 & 14 Mini-review

1. Language check

A Compare each of the two things. Write sentences.

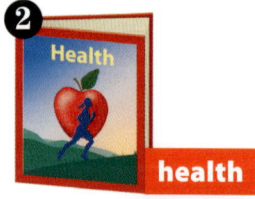

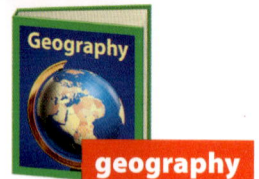

1. soccer / tennis
2. health / geography
3. Sydney / Rome
4. Canada / the United States
5. hamburgers / hot dogs
6. cats / dogs

1. (difficult) *Soccer is more difficult than tennis.*
   OR *Tennis is more difficult than soccer.*
2. (important) _____
3. (beautiful) _____
4. (interesting) _____
5. (delicious) _____
6. (intelligent) _____

B Compare the two sports using the words in the box or your own ideas.

☐ challenging ☑ dangerous ☐ difficult ☐ exciting ☐ interesting

1. *Surfing is more dangerous than skateboarding.*
2. _____
3. _____
4. _____
5. _____

surfing

skateboarding

48   Unit 4

C Use the cues to make sentences.

1. Race cars / fast / bumper cars
   Race cars are faster than bumper cars.

2. A soccer ball / big / a golf ball
   _____

3. Theme parks / exciting / school festivals
   _____

4. Portugal / small / France
   _____

5. MP3 players / popular / CD players
   _____

6. New York City / busy / Chicago
   _____

7. Libraries / relaxing / malls
   _____

8. English / useful / science
   _____

2. Listening

Joe writes Penny an e-mail from camp. Listen and circle the correct words.

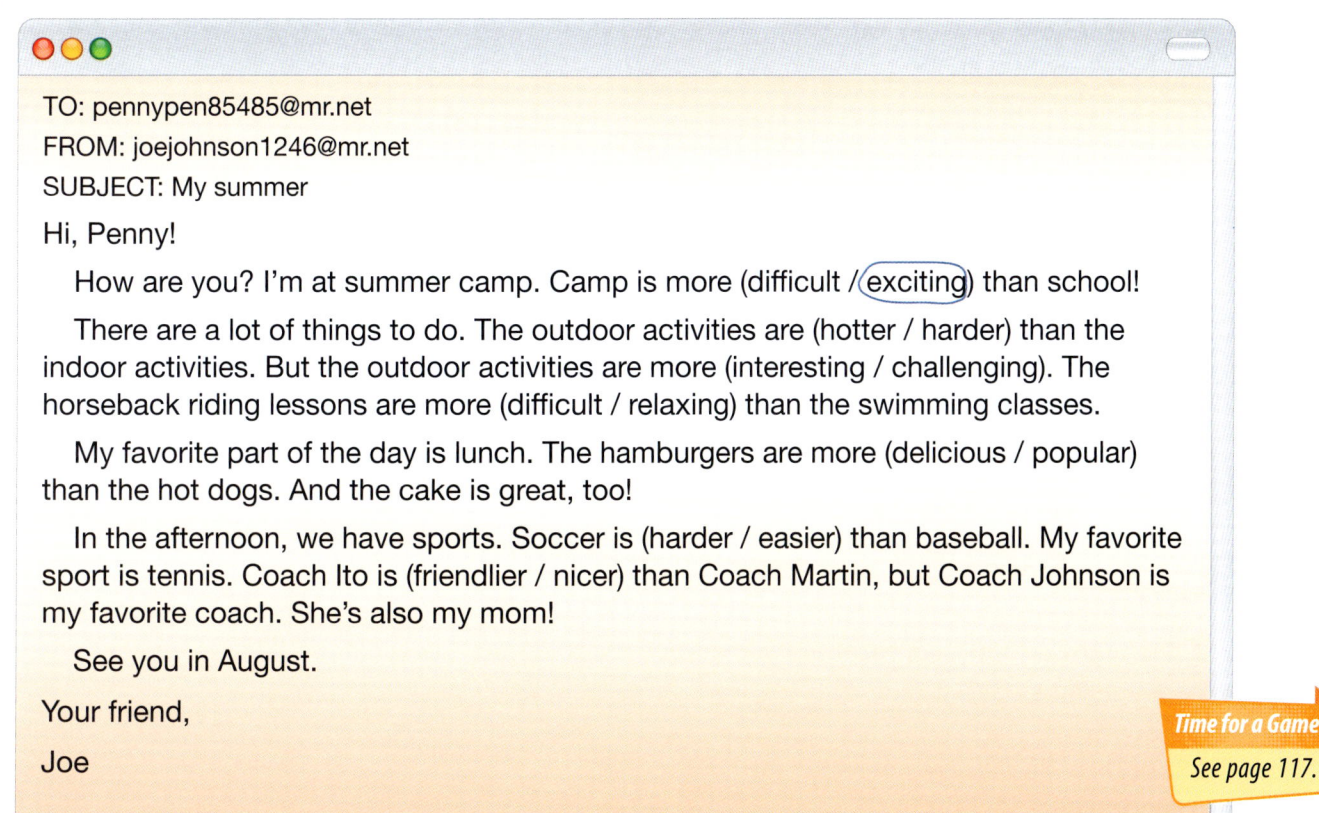

TO: pennypen85485@mr.net
FROM: joejohnson1246@mr.net
SUBJECT: My summer

Hi, Penny!

How are you? I'm at summer camp. Camp is more (difficult / (exciting)) than school!

There are a lot of things to do. The outdoor activities are (hotter / harder) than the indoor activities. But the outdoor activities are more (interesting / challenging). The horseback riding lessons are more (difficult / relaxing) than the swimming classes.

My favorite part of the day is lunch. The hamburgers are more (delicious / popular) than the hot dogs. And the cake is great, too!

In the afternoon, we have sports. Soccer is (harder / easier) than baseball. My favorite sport is tennis. Coach Ito is (friendlier / nicer) than Coach Martin, but Coach Johnson is my favorite coach. She's also my mom!

See you in August.

Your friend,

Joe

Time for a Game?
See page 117.

Lesson 15: World trivia

1. Language focus

A Read these pages from a world trivia book. Complete the sentences. Listen and check. Then practice.

Superlative adjectives: -est

What's **the highest** mountain in the world?
Mount Everest is **the highest** mountain in the world.
Mount Everest is **the highest** mountain.

DO YOU KNOW ABOUT THESE WORLD RECORDS?

1. Mount Everest is the _highest_ (high) mountain in the world. It's 29,035 feet (8,850 meters) high.

2. Venus is the _____ (hot) planet in the solar system. It can be 900 degrees Fahrenheit (482 degrees Celsius).

3. The dwarf gecko is the _____ (short) reptile in the world. It's only 0.63 inches (1.6 centimeters) long.

4. The blue whale is the _____ (heavy) animal in the world. It weighs about 110 tons (99,790 kilograms).

5. Vatican City is the _____ (small) country in the world. It's 0.15 square miles (0.4 square kilometers). About 880 people live there.

6. The Akashi Kaikyo Bridge in Japan is the _____ (long) bridge in the world. It's about 6,532 feet (1,991 meters) long.

B Write the superlative form of each adjective.

1. high _highest_
2. long _____
3. cute _____
4. short _____
5. cold _____
6. large _____

Spelling superlatives

small → small**est**
big → big**gest**
late → lat**est**
heavy → heav**iest**

50 Unit 4

C Look at the photos. Write questions and answers. Then listen and check.

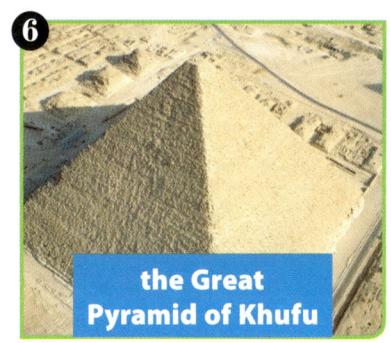

1 coastal redwood
2 the cheetah
3 the Andes
4 the bee hummingbird
5 Ojos del Salado
6 the Great Pyramid of Khufu

1. (tall / tree) **Q:** What's the tallest tree in the world?

   A: The coastal redwood is the tallest tree in the world.

2. (fast / land animal) **Q:** _____

   A: _____

3. (long / mountain range) **Q:** _____

   A: _____

4. (light / bird) **Q:** _____

   A: _____

5. (high / volcano) **Q:** _____

   A: _____

6. (large / pyramid) **Q:** _____

   A: _____

2. Listening

Three people are playing a trivia game. Listen to each question. Check (✓) the correct answer.

1.	✓ the Statue of Liberty	☐ the Eiffel Tower	☐ the Empire State Building
2.	☐ an Airbus A380	☐ a Boeing 747	☐ a McDonnell Douglas MD-11
3.	☐ the United States	☐ Russia	☐ Canada
4.	☐ Seoul	☐ Tokyo	☐ Mexico City
5.	☐ Australia	☐ Antarctica	☐ Europe

Comparisons 51

Lesson 16 — The most

1. Language focus

A Read Mr. In-the-Know's Web site. Then listen and practice.

T.60

Superlative adjectives: *the most*

Use *the most* with adjectives of two or more syllables:
expensive → the most expensive
What's **the most expensive** city in the world?
The most expensive city in the world is Moscow.
The most expensive city is Moscow.
Moscow is **the most expensive** city.

http:// www.mr.in-the-know.com

Ask
Mr. In-the-Know

Here's what I think . . .

Q: What's the most expensive city in the world?
A: Moscow, Russia is the most expensive city in the world. A cup of coffee costs more than $5.00!

Q: What's the most populous country in the world?
A: The most populous country is China. There are more than one billion people.

Q: What's the most thrilling city in the world?
A: Orlando, Florida is the most thrilling city. There are more than 13 theme parks there.

Q: What's the most interesting city in the world?
A: Washington, D.C. is the most interesting city. Both the largest museum and the largest library in the world are there.

B Write questions and answers about places in your country. Use the adjectives in the box.

☑ beautiful ☐ crowded ☐ expensive ☐ interesting ☐ popular

1. *What's the most beautiful city in Brazil? The most beautiful city in Brazil is Rio.*
   OR *The most beautiful city is Rio.*   OR *Rio is the most beautiful city.*
2. _____
3. _____
4. _____
5. _____

2. Word power

A Check (✓) the word that does NOT belong in each list.

1. the most thrilling
   - ☐ movie
   - ✓ sand
   - ☐ book

2. the most crowded
   - ☐ sport
   - ☐ city
   - ☐ country

3. the most popular
   - ☐ music store
   - ☐ café
   - ☐ kitchen

4. the most expensive
   - ☐ shop
   - ☐ restaurant
   - ☐ library

5. the most beautiful
   - ☐ beach
   - ☐ flower
   - ☐ ball

6. the most famous
   - ☐ movie star
   - ☐ singer
   - ☐ dining room

7. the most interesting
   - ☐ bathroom
   - ☐ book
   - ☐ museum

8. the most dangerous
   - ☐ table
   - ☐ city
   - ☐ animal

B Write sentences using *the most*. Use ideas from Part A or your own ideas.

1. The most popular café in my town is Carrine's Café.
2.
3.
4.
5.
6.
7.
8.

3. Speaking

A What's in your classmate's bag? Complete the questions. Then interview your classmate.

	Interview questions	Answers
1. important	What's the most important thing in your bag?	
2. beautiful		
3. expensive		
4. interesting		
5. useful		

B Share your classmate's answers with the class.

> Money is the most important thing in Monica's bag.

Comparisons 53

UNIT 4 Get Connected

Read

A Read the facts quickly. Check (✓) the words you find.

☑ the fastest ☐ larger ☐ longer ☐ the oldest ☐ the slowest ☐ the youngest

Fun Amusement Park Facts

- The biggest amusement park in the world is Walt Disney World in Florida in the U.S. About 54,000 people work there.

- The oldest amusement park in the world is Bakken in Denmark. It **opened** in 1583.

- Cedar Point in Ohio is one of the oldest amusement parks in the U.S. The park's first roller coaster opened in 1892 and **traveled** 10 **miles per hour** (16 kilometers per hour).

- Kingda Ka at Six Flags Great Adventure in New Jersey in the U.S. is the tallest and fastest **outdoor** roller coaster in the world. It's 456 feet (139 meters) high, and it goes 128 miles per hour (206 kilometers per hour).

- The Steel Dragon 2000 roller coaster in Japan is slower than Kingda Ka, but it's longer. It's the longest outdoor roller coaster in the world. It's 8,133 feet (2,479 meters) long.

- What amusement park in the world has the most **rides**? Cedar Point in Ohio. It has 75 rides.

More Vocabulary Practice? See page 123.

B 🎧 T.61 Read the facts slowly. Check your answers in Part A.

C Answer the questions.

1. What's the biggest amusement park in the world?
   The biggest amusement park in the world is Walt Disney World in Florida.

2. What's the oldest amusement park in the world?
   _____

3. What's the fastest outdoor roller coaster in the world?
   _____

4. What's the longest outdoor roller coaster?
   _____

5. What amusement park has the most rides?
   _____

I love roller coasters!

Listen

A Lisa and Kevin talk about amusement parks. Listen and write *True* or *False*. Then correct the false statements.

1. Lisa ~~went to Kevin's house yesterday but he wasn't home~~. _False_
   called Kevin yesterday but no one answered.
2. Kevin went to an amusement park with his cousins. _____
3. Kevin likes amusement parks a lot. _____
4. Lisa thinks bumper cars are more exciting than roller coasters. _____
5. Kevin and Lisa think amusement parks are expensive. _____

B What do you think? Write *I agree* or *I disagree*. Give reasons.

1. It's better to go somewhere to celebrate your birthday than to celebrate it at home. _____
2. Roller coasters are safe. _____
3. Expensive food always tastes good. _____
4. Very young children should go on roller coasters. _____

Your turn

Write

A Think of a place you went for fun. Answer the questions.

1. What's the name of the place? _____
2. When did you go there? _____
3. What was the most exciting thing you did there? _____
4. What was the most boring thing you did there? _____
5. What were the most expensive things there? _____

B Write a paragraph about the place. Use the answers in Part A to help you.

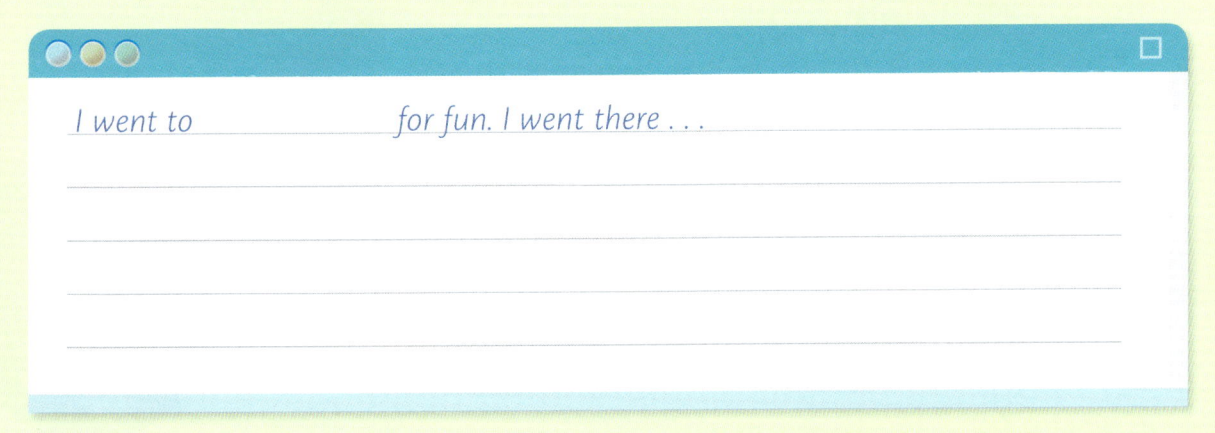

I went to _____ for fun. I went there . . .

UNIT 4 Review

Language chart review

Comparative adjectives

short → short**er**   Ellie is **shorter than** Paula.
busy → bus**ier**   Ms. Peterson is **busier than** Ms. Stevens.

Superlative adjectives: -est

What's **the longest** river in the United States?
The Mississippi River is **the longest** river in the United States.

A Rewrite the sentences so they are true.

1. Whales are bigger than dolphins.
   (small) *Dolphins are smaller than whales.*

2. Dolphins are slower than whales.
   (fast) _____

3. Sawsharks are smaller than white sharks.
   (large) _____

4. Dolphins are lighter than whales.
   (heavy) _____

5. Black bears are shorter than grizzly bears.
   (tall) _____

B Complete the conversations with the superlative forms of the adjectives in the box.

☐ fast   ☑ large   ☐ slow   ☐ tall

1. **A** What's ___the largest___ mammal in the ocean?
   B The whale is ___the largest___ mammal in the ocean.

2. **A** What's _____ mammal on land?
   B The cheetah is _____ mammal on land.
   The cheetah is even faster than some cars!

3. **A** What's _____ mammal in the world?
   B The giraffe is _____ mammal in the world.
   Many giraffes are more than 16½ feet (5 meters) tall.

4. **A** What's _____ fish in the ocean?
   B The sea horse is _____ fish in the ocean.
   It only travels 0.01 miles (0.016 kilometers) per hour.

Language chart review

Comparative adjectives: more ... than

expensive → more expensive
difficult → more difficult

Cars are **more expensive than** bikes.
English is **more difficult than** science.

Superlative adjectives: the most

What's **the most famous** bridge in California?
The most famous bridge in California is the Golden Gate Bridge.
The most famous bridge is the Golden Gate Bridge.
The Golden Gate Bridge is **the most famous** bridge.

C Look at the results in Part 1 of the class survey. Then write sentences with comparative adjectives and *more*.

Mr. King's Class Survey – Topics and Votes

PART 1				PART 2		
Movies: comedies 17, dramas 1	**Sports:** tennis 14, soccer 4	**Desserts:** cookies 18, cake 0	**Music:** pop 11, hip-hop 7	**Popular singers:** Beyoncé 9, Carrie Underwood 6, Justin Timberlake 3	**Delicious snacks:** chips 12, fruit 4, vegetables 2	**Thrilling sports:** waterskiing 10, soccer 6, skateboarding 2

1. (movies / entertaining) *Comedies are more entertaining than dramas.*
2. (sports / exciting) _____
3. (desserts / delicious) _____
4. (music / popular) _____

D Now look at the results in Part 2 of the class survey. Write questions and answers using superlatives.

1. **Q:** *Who's the most popular singer?*
   A: *Beyoncé is the most popular singer.*
2. **Q:** _____
   A: _____
3. **Q:** _____
   A: _____

Take another look!

Circle T (true) or F (false).

1. Comparative adjectives end in *-est*.   T   F
2. We use *the most* in superlative questions and statements.   T   F
3. We only use *-er* with two-syllable words that end in *y*.   T   F

Time for the Theme Project?
See page 129.

Comparisons 57

Lesson 17 Yoga class

1. Word power

A Andrea joined a yoga class to make her body more relaxed and flexible. How many parts of the body do you know? Listen and practice.

finger(s) · hand · thumb · wrist · arm · elbow · back · nose · mouth · eye · stomach · neck · head · ear · face · knee · leg · foot / feet · heel · ankle · toe(s)

B Close your book. Ask a classmate to name and point to the parts of the body labeled in Part A.

You Point to your neck.
Classmate This is my neck. Point to your feet.
You These are my feet. Point to your . . .

UNIT 5 Your Health

58

2. Language focus

A Read the introduction to Andrea's new yoga book. Then listen and practice.

Do you want to make your body stronger? Would you like to move more flexibly? Try yoga. It's a great way to exercise, and it helps relax your body and mind. Yoga can improve your health. It can help you play sports. Yoga can even help you think more clearly!

Do each pose slowly and carefully. Don't move too fast. Hard, fast movements can hurt your body. Wear loose clothing so you can move comfortably, and don't eat before you practice. What's the most important thing? Remember to breathe regularly! And don't forget to relax peacefully for a few minutes after you finish. Practice patiently every day, and enjoy a healthier life!

> **Adverbs of manner**
>
> Adverbs are often formed by adding -ly to the adjective form of a word.
> slow → slowly
> quiet → quietly
> Do each pose **slowly** and **carefully**.
> Practice **patiently** every day.
>
> Note:
> Change y to i and add -ly:
> happy → happily
> Drop silent final e and add -ly:
> flexible → flexibly
> Exception:
> fast → fast

B Complete this advice from Andrea's yoga teacher by changing the adjectives to adverbs. Then listen and check.

1. Dress _comfortably_ (comfortable).
2. Don't move too _____ (fast).
3. Practice _____ (regular).
4. Choose your teacher _____ (careful).

C Match the sentences from Part B to the sentences below.

1. _Practice regularly._ — Try to do it every day.
2. _____ — It's important to go slowly.
3. _____ — You need a good instructor.
4. _____ — Never wear shoes or a belt.

3. Speaking

Think of an activity and choose an adverb from the box. Act out the activity in the manner of the adverb. Your classmates guess what you are doing.

Classmate 1 Are you surfing happily?
You No, I'm not.
Classmate 2 Are you dancing crazily?
You Yes, I am.

carefully   correctly   crazily
happily   quickly   quietly
sadly   slowly

Your Health

Lesson 18: I don't feel well.

1. Word power

A These people don't feel well. What's the matter? Listen and practice.

1. a cold
2. an earache
3. the flu
4. a headache
5. a sore throat
6. allergies

B The people in Part A are following their doctors' advice. Complete the advice with words from Part A.

Doctors' Advice*

1. For ___the flu___, try chicken soup or some soda and crackers, and stay in bed.
2. For _____, use warm eardrops every four hours.
3. For _____, take some cold medicine, and drink a lot of water.
4. For _____, try hot tea with lemon – and try not to talk too much!
5. For _____, take some allergy pills. Use eyedrops, too!
6. For _____, take two aspirin. Try to rest in a quiet place with your eyes closed.

*This advice should not replace the advice of your own doctor.

2. Language focus

A Josh calls Felipe to invite him to a basketball game. Listen and practice.

Josh Hi, Felipe. It's Josh. Do you want to go to the basketball game tonight?

Felipe No, thanks. I have a bad cold. What do you do when you have a cold?

Josh I take cold medicine and drink a lot of orange juice. I also stay in bed.

Felipe I do, too. I can stay in bed and watch videos. When I don't feel well, my dad rents them for me.

Josh That's really nice. My dad doesn't do that when I have a cold . . .

Felipe Well, he does a lot of other nice things for you. I bet he's driving you to the game tonight, right?

> **Clauses with *when***
>
> What do you do **when you have a cold**?
> I take cold medicine **when I have a cold**.
> **When I have a cold**, I take cold medicine.
> I take cold medicine.

B Write questions and answers about the pictures. Use *when* in the questions. Then listen and check.

1. **Q:** *What does she do when she has a headache?*
   A: *When she has a headache, she takes aspirin.*
   OR *She takes aspirin when she has a headache.* OR *She takes aspirin.*
2. **Q:** _____
   A: _____
3. **Q:** _____
   A: _____
4. **Q:** _____
   A: _____

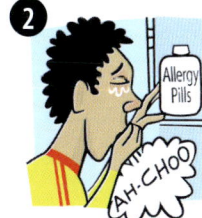

3. Listening

A Listen to the radio health program. According to the doctor, do these people do the correct things when they have health problems? Write *Yes* or *No*.

1. Diego _____   2. Stella _____   3. Craig _____   4. Sheila _____

B Talk to a classmate about what you do when you have health problems.

> What do you do when you have the flu?

> I usually go to the doctor.

Your Health 61

Lessons 17 & 18 Mini-review

1. Language check

A Readers sent their special remedies to *Teen Health Magazine*. Read the remedies. Then write sentences starting with *When*.

What special remedies do you use when you are sick?*

1. Sometimes I have insomnia. I can't sleep. I drink warm milk and read something boring. Then I can go to sleep easily!
   – *Liz*

2. For a sore throat, I eat a banana before bed. I always feel better in the morning.
   – *Tommy*

3. For an earache, I put drops of warm olive oil in my ears. It sounds strange, but it really works!
   – *Marta*

4. For a headache, I put a warm cloth on my head.
   – *Jeff*

5. I don't really like orange juice, but I drink a lot of it when I have a cold.
   – *Anita*

6. To fight the flu, I drink hot water with lemon. My family always does this. Why don't you try it?
   – *Ray*

*This advice should not replace the advice of your own doctor.

1. *When Liz has insomnia, she drinks warm milk and reads something boring.*
2. _____
3. _____
4. _____
5. _____
6. _____

B Write the adverbs of manner for each adjective.

1. comfortable *comfortably*
2. correct _____
3. patient _____
4. peaceful _____
5. regular _____
6. happy _____
7. safe _____
8. quiet _____
9. slow _____
10. careful _____

62 Unit 5

C Use the adverbs in Part B to complete the health and fitness advice.

1. Choose snacks _carefully_. Think about what you want to eat. Do you really need junk food?
2. Eat _____. When people eat too quickly, they usually eat too much.
3. Sit and stand _____. The right way is to keep your back and shoulders straight.
4. Exercise _____. Do something active for 30 minutes every day.
5. Play sports _____. Use the right equipment, and follow the rules of the game.
6. It's not healthy to be frustrated when you have to wait for something. It's good to wait _____.
7. It's not good to be uncomfortable when you study. Sit _____ at your desk.
8. Live your life _____! It's not good to be sad.
9. Talk _____ when you are in the library.
10. After a long day at school, relax _____ before bed time. Then you can go to sleep easily.

2. Listening

Dr. Sita talks to Melanie about her problems. What does Dr. Sita say? Listen and number the sentences in the correct order.

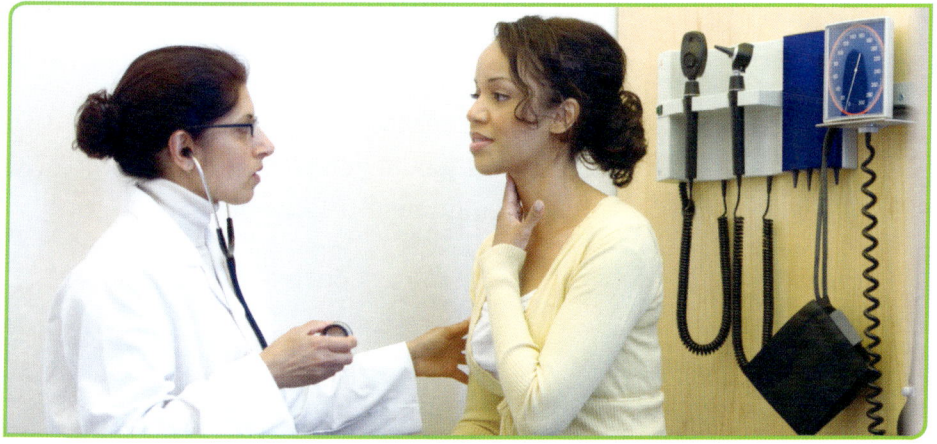

____ You worry less when you're relaxed.
____ You need to sit comfortably when you study.
_1_ When you don't sleep regularly, you get tired.
____ Take two aspirin when you get a headache.
____ When you're tired in the afternoon, eat a healthy snack.
____ When you study for an hour, get up and move around for a few minutes.

Time for a Game?
See page 118.

Lesson 19 — Are you healthy?

1. Language focus

A Andrea completes the online quiz. Listen and underline her answers. Then practice.

T.71

> **How often . . . ? and time expressions**
>
> **How often** do you eat vegetables?
> I eat vegetables **twice a day**.
> I **never** eat vegetables.
>
> every day / week / month / year
> three times a day / week / month / year
> twice a day / week / month / year
> once a day / week / month / year

http:// www.how-healthy-are-you?

How healthy are you?

1 How often do you drink water?
- three or more times a day 3
- twice a day 2
- once a day 1
- never 0

2 How often do you eat vegetables?
- three or more times a day 3
- twice a day 2
- once a day 1
- never 0

3 How often do you drink soda?
- never 3
- one to three times a week 2
- four to six times a week 1
- every day 0

4 How often do you eat sweets?
- never 3
- once or twice a week 2
- three to five times a week 1
- every day 0

5 How often do you exercise?
- every day 3
- four to six times a week 2
- one to three times a week 1
- never 0

6 How often do you brush your teeth?
- three times a day 3
- twice a day 2
- once a day 1
- never 0

7 How often do you get eight or more hours of sleep?
- six to seven times a week 3
- four to five times a week 2
- one to three times a week 1
- never 0

8 How often do you wash your hands?
- three or more times a day 3
- twice a day 2
- once a day 1
- never 0

Add the numbers next to your answers to get your score!

- **20 – 24 points** Great! You care a lot about your health. Keep up the good work!
- **15 – 19 points** You do a lot for your health, but you can do a little more. Think about exercise and eating habits.
- **10 – 14 points** You need to think more about your health. Get more sleep and exercise, and eat better foods.
- **0 – 9 points** You don't take good care of your health. You can do better! Start today!

B Take the health quiz. Circle your answers. What's your score?

C Write how often you do the things in Part A. Then tell a classmate.

I exercise about six times a week.

1. _____
2. _____
3. _____
4. _____
5. _____
6. _____
7. _____
8. _____

I exercise about six times a week.

That's great. I exercise about three times a week.

2. Speaking

A Write *How often* questions about other healthy activities. Use the activities in the box or your own ideas.

dance	have sports practice
drink water	ride a bicycle
go to the doctor for a checkup	run
have gym class	swim

How often do you have gym class?

1. _____
2. _____
3. _____
4. _____
5. _____
6. _____
7. _____
8. _____

B Ask a classmate your questions.

How often do you have gym class?

I have gym class three times a week.

Your Health

Lesson 20 — Teen health tips

1. Word power

A Read the health tips in the box, and write them above the correct advice. Then listen and practice.

T.72

- ☐ Be active.
- ☐ Don't skip breakfast.
- ☐ Protect your skin.
- ☑ Challenge your brain.
- ☐ Get your vitamins and minerals.
- ☐ Reduce stress.
- ☐ Don't eat junk food.
- ☐ Prevent cavities.

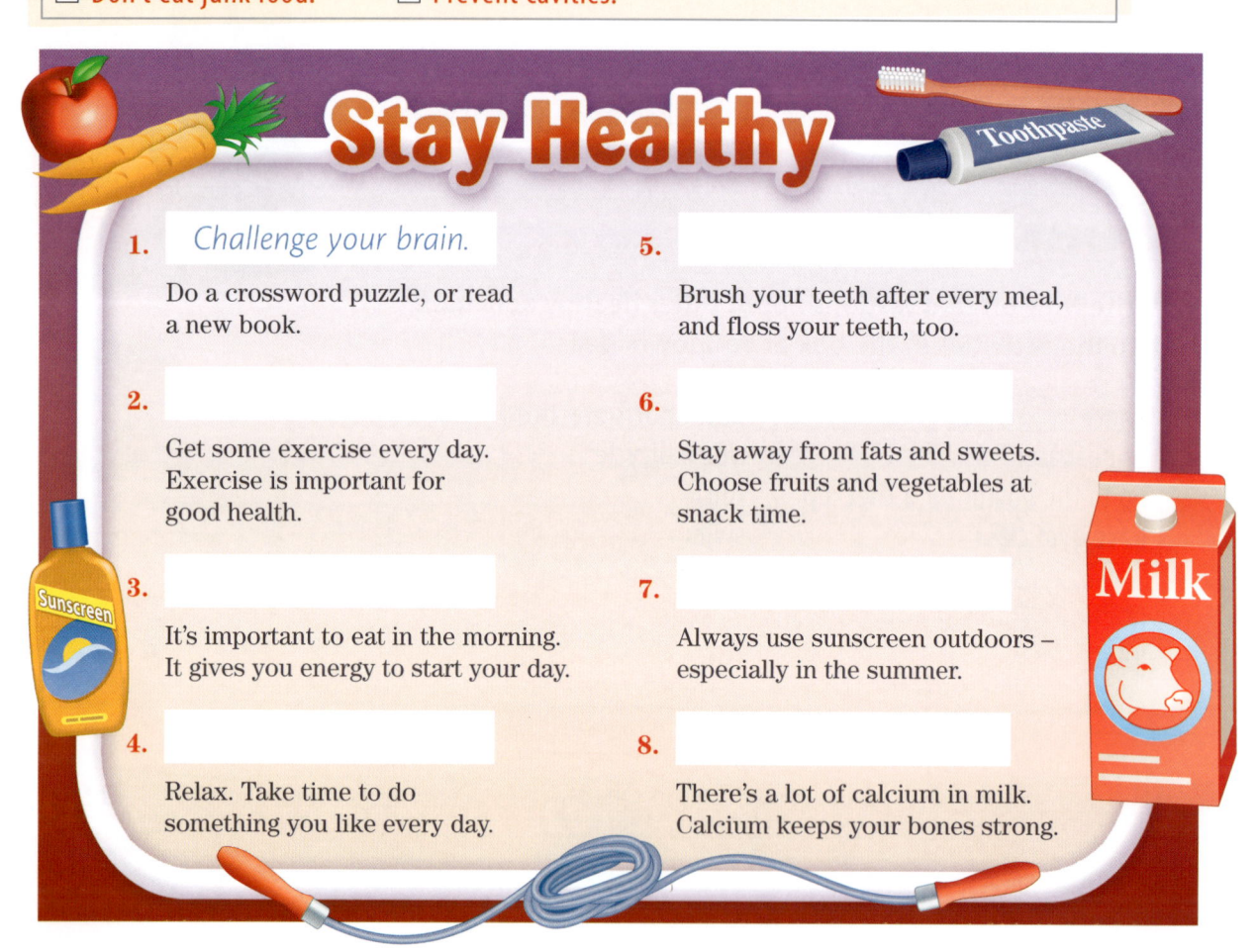

Stay Healthy

1. *Challenge your brain.*
   Do a crossword puzzle, or read a new book.

2. _____
   Get some exercise every day. Exercise is important for good health.

3. _____
   It's important to eat in the morning. It gives you energy to start your day.

4. _____
   Relax. Take time to do something you like every day.

5. _____
   Brush your teeth after every meal, and floss your teeth, too.

6. _____
   Stay away from fats and sweets. Choose fruits and vegetables at snack time.

7. _____
   Always use sunscreen outdoors – especially in the summer.

8. _____
   There's a lot of calcium in milk. Calcium keeps your bones strong.

B Which health tips do you follow? Write sentences. Then tell your classmates.

I challenge my brain. I read a lot of new books.

1. _____
2. _____
3. _____
4. _____

I challenge my brain. I read a lot of new books. I . . .

66   Unit 5

2. Language focus

should / shouldn't

You **should** eat a good breakfast.
You **shouldn't** skip breakfast.

A Josh did not eat breakfast. He is running out the door. Listen and practice.

T.73

Amy Josh, wait. Don't go yet. You should eat a good breakfast.
Josh I don't have time! I'm late!
Amy Josh, you shouldn't skip breakfast. It gives you energy.
Josh But I'm not hungry. I had some pizza at 11:30 last night.
Amy At 11:30? What time did you go to bed?
Josh Oh, at about 1:00 a.m.
Amy Josh, you shouldn't stay up so late. You're not taking care of yourself.
Josh Sure I am. I had to study for a test. I want to get to school early so that I can study a little more.
Amy How are you getting to school?
Josh I planned to walk, but actually, now I have to *run*!
Amy Well, good. You should be more active.

B Rewrite the sentences. Use *should* or *shouldn't*. Then listen and check.

T.74

1. Don't skip breakfast. *You shouldn't skip breakfast.*
2. Prevent cavities. *You should prevent cavities.*
3. Be active. _____
4. Don't eat junk food. _____
5. Challenge your brain. _____
6. Protect your skin. _____
7. Reduce stress. _____
8. Get your vitamins and minerals. _____

3. Listening

The school nurse is talking to students. Complete her health advice with *should* or *shouldn't*.

T.75

1. To Nadia: You _____ eat lunch.
2. To Lenny: You _____ go home.
3. To Beth: You _____ take yoga.
4. To Sylvia: You _____ stay indoors.

Your Health

UNIT 5 Get Connected

Read

A Read the article quickly. Write the names of five martial arts.

1. _____ 3. _____ 5. _____
2. _____ 4. _____

Martial arts for everyone

The study of **martial arts** is popular around the world. Martial arts are good for **self-defense** and they're good exercise. The **philosophy** of martial arts can help people live more happily and peacefully.

There are many kinds of martial arts. Karate, aikido, and judo are from Japan. Tae kwon do is from Korea, and Capoeira is popular in Brazil. Kung fu and tai chi are two popular martial arts from China.

The study of martial arts has many **benefits**. Martial arts improve flexibility and make people stronger. Also, the skills and **discipline** people learn doing a martial art often improve **self-esteem**. Many people study martial arts to learn self-defense.

Martial arts can be a lot of fun. So, try a martial art. With martial arts schools in almost every country, you can **probably** find one near you.

More Vocabulary Practice? See page 124.

B T.76 Read the article slowly. Check your answers in Part A.

C Are these statements true or false? Write *True* or *False*. Then correct the false statements.

1. Martial arts aren't a good form of exercise.
   False. Martial arts are good for self-defense and they're good exercise.

2. Karate, aikido, and judo are all from Japan.
   _____

3. When you practice martial arts regularly, they improve your flexibility.
   _____

4. You should try a martial art to improve your self-esteem and have fun.
   _____

5. There are martial arts schools only in Japan.
   _____

You should try Capoeira.

Listen

A 🎧 T.77 **Alex and Isabel talk about Capoeira. Listen and answer the questions.**

1. What's Capoeira? _It's a martial art._
2. How often does Isabel have class? _____
3. Is Isabel strong? _____
4. Does Isabel always do her homework now? _____
5. Does Alex want to try Capoeira? _____

B What do you think? Answer the questions. Give reasons.

1. Do you think doing martial arts is a cool hobby?

   _____

2. Would you like to try a martial arts class?

   _____

3. Do you believe that martial arts can help improve your grades?

   _____

4. Do you think it's a good idea to learn self-defense?

   _____

Your turn

Write

A Think about a sport or activity that teaches discipline. Answer the questions.

1. What's the name of the sport / activity? _____
2. Where's it from? _____
3. What are its benefits? _____
4. What kind of equipment do you need? _____
5. How often should you practice this sport / activity? _____

B Write an article for a teen magazine about sports or activities that teens learn discipline from. Use the answers in Part A to help you.

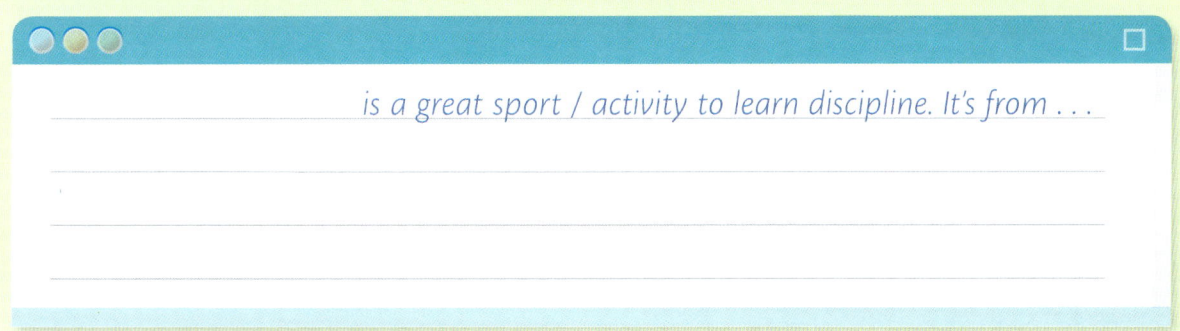

_____ *is a great sport / activity to learn discipline. It's from . . .*

Your Health

UNIT 5 Review

Language chart review

Adverbs of manner

quick → quickly
quiet → quietly
Please walk **quickly** and **quietly**.

Exception:
fast → fast
Don't drive too **fast**.

***How often...?* and time expressions**

How often do you eat fruit?
I eat fruit **twice a day**.
I **never** eat fruit.

A Complete the sentences by changing the adjectives to adverbs.

This is Tonya. She's 14. She takes dance classes four times a week. She practices ___regularly___ (regular). Tonya tries to get ten hours of sleep at least six nights a week. But sometimes, when she's tired, she doesn't dance as _____ (quick) or as _____ (careful) as she should. Tonya always stretches before class so that she can move _____ (slow) and _____ (easy). And, she always dances _____ (correct) so that she doesn't hurt herself. Tonya eats healthy food every day, but she eats dessert three times a week.

B Complete the questions. Then answer the questions with the information in Part A.

1. **Q:** _How often_ does Tonya take dance classes?
   A: _She takes dance classes four times a week._

2. **Q:** _____ does Tonya stretch before class?
   A: _____

3. **Q:** _____ does Tonya eat healthy food?
   A: _____

4. **Q:** _____ does Tonya get ten hours of sleep?
   A: _____

5. **Q:** _____ does Tonya eat dessert?
   A: _____

Language chart review

Clauses with *when*

When I have a headache, I take aspirin.
I take aspirin when I have a headache.
What do you do when you have a headache?
   I rest in a quiet place.

should / shouldn't

You **should** sleep eight hours a night.
You **shouldn't** stay up late.

C Look at the chart, and complete the conversations. Use clauses with *when*.

	Andrew	Jessica	Dr. Melvin
a cold	skip breakfast	eat junk food	take cold medicine
the flu	go swimming	go shopping	stay in bed
a sore throat	drink milk shakes	drink soda	drink tea with lemon

1. **Dr. Melvin** (you / a cold) *What do you do when you have a cold?*
   Andrew *When I have a cold, I skip breakfast.* OR *I skip breakfast when I have a cold.* OR *I skip breakfast.*
   Jessica _____
2. **Dr. Melvin** (you / the flu) _____
   Andrew _____
   Jessica _____
3. **Dr. Melvin** (you / a sore throat) _____
   Andrew _____
   Jessica _____

D Dr. Melvin doesn't agree with Andrew's and Jessica's remedies. Look at Part C again. Write the doctor's advice. Use *should* and *shouldn't*.

1. (Andrew / a cold) *Andrew shouldn't skip breakfast. He should take cold medicine.*
2. (Jessica / the flu) _____
3. (Andrew / a sore throat) _____
4. (Jessica / a cold) _____
5. (Andrew / the flu) _____

Take another look!

Circle the correct answer.

Which sentence means the same as "Don't talk."?
   a. You should talk.   b. You shouldn't talk.   c. I never talk.

Time for the Theme Project?
See page 130.

Lesson 21: School fund-raiser

1. Language focus

A Look at the poster. Josh and Andrea talk about raising money for their school. Listen and practice.

T.78

Wells International School Fund-raiser

Do chores to raise money for our school!

- wash windows
- do yard work
- walk dogs
- babysit
- wash cars
- work at the bake sale

Sign up in the cafeteria today!

Josh Hey, Andrea. Look at the poster. Are you going to do anything for the fund-raiser?
Andrea Yeah. I'm going to do yard work.
Josh Really? Is Luigi going to do yard work, too?
Andrea No, he isn't. He's going to wash windows. How about you? Are you going to sign up for anything?
Josh I'm going to sign up, but I'm not going to wash windows! I'm not going to do yard work, either. It's too much work.
Andrea Are you going to walk dogs? That sounds easy.
Josh No, I'm not. I'd like to babysit or work at the bake sale.
Andrea Well, I think you should work at the bake sale. Babysitting is hard work!

---

be going to

I'**m going to** do yard work.
He'**s going to** wash windows.
Are you **going to** walk dogs?
Yes, I am. / No, I'm not.
Is Luigi **going to** do yard work?
Yes, he is. / No, he isn't.

UNIT 6 Special Events

72

B What will students do for the fund-raiser? Write sentences. Then listen and check.

School Fund-raiser					
Babysit	Do yard work	Walk dogs	Wash cars	Wash windows	Work at the bake sale
Mandy	Andrea	Felipe	Vince	Justin	Josh
Kevin			Emily	Luigi	Marta

1. (Mandy and Kevin) *Mandy and Kevin are going to babysit.*
2. (Andrea) _____
3. (Vince and Emily) _____
4. (Felipe) _____
5. (Josh and Marta) _____
6. (Justin and Luigi) _____

C Read the sign-up sheet in Part B again. Write questions and short answers. Then listen and check.

1. (Andrea / babysit) **Q:** *Is Andrea going to babysit?* **A:** *No, she isn't.*
2. (Felipe / walk dogs) **Q:** _____ **A:** _____
3. (Justin and Luigi / wash cars) **Q:** _____ **A:** _____
4. (Emily / wash windows) **Q:** _____ **A:** _____

2. Pronunciation Reduction of *going to*

Notice how *going to* is reduced to *gonna*. Listen and practice. Then practice the conversation on page 72 focusing on *going to (gonna)*.

Q: Are you **gonna** wash cars?
A: No, I'm not. I'm **gonna** wash windows.

Q: Is she **gonna** babysit?
A: No, she isn't. She's **gonna** work at the bake sale.

3. Listening

Andrea and her brother and sister have a birthday surprise for their father. They are going to do chores for him. Listen and match the chores to the correct names.

1. Fernando *d*
2. Bruna _____
3. Andrea _____

a. do yard work
b. clean the garage
c. wash the car
d. walk the dog
e. organize books
f. make dinner

Special Events

Lesson 22: A farewell party

1. Word power

A Mrs. Delgado is leaving Wells International School. Her students are planning a farewell party. Complete their to-do list with the verbs in the box. Then listen and practice.

- ☐ decorate
- ☐ perform
- ☐ serve
- ☑ sign
- ☐ make
- ☐ pour
- ☐ set up
- ☐ wrap

Mrs. Delgado's Farewell Party To-Do List

Names	Things to do
Everyone	1. _sign_ the card
Andrea	2. _____ the drinks
Amy, José	3. _____ the snack table
Mandy	4. _____ the gift
Everyone	5. _____ a special dance
Everyone	6. _____ the cafeteria
Felipe	7. _____ a speech
Josh	8. _____ the pizza

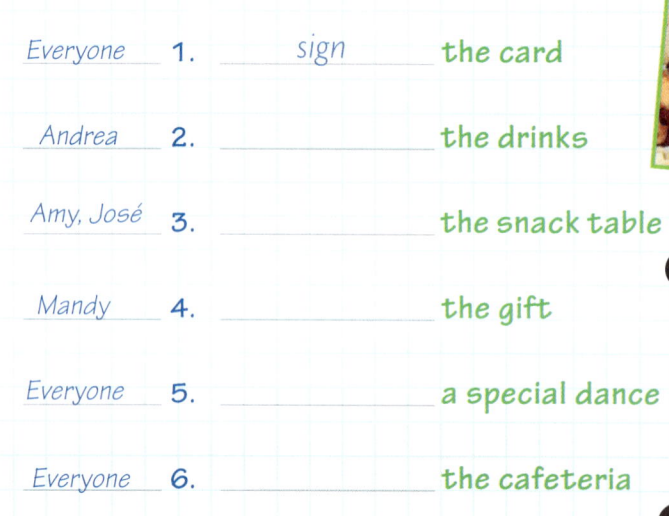

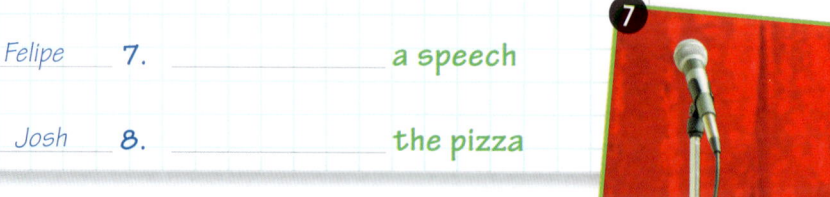

B When will students do the activities in Part A? Complete the chart.

Before the party	At the party
sign the card	pour the drinks

2. Language focus

A Luigi asks Mandy about the party plans. Listen and practice.

Luigi Hi, Mandy. Sorry I missed the meeting about Mrs. Delgado's farewell party.
Mandy That's OK. I think we're all set.
Luigi Where are we going to have the party?
Mandy In the cafeteria.
Luigi Why do we need so much space? What are we going to do?
Mandy We're going to perform a special dance.
Luigi Great! What are we going to eat?
Mandy Pizza. We're going to eat right after the speech.
Luigi Who's going to make the speech?
Mandy Felipe is.

> **Wh- questions with *be going to***
>
> **Who's going to** make the speech?
> Felipe **is going to** make the speech.
> Felipe **is**.
> Felipe.
> **What are we going to** eat?
> We**'re going to** eat pizza.
> Pizza.
> **Where are we going to** have the party?
> We**'re going to** have it in the cafeteria.
> In the cafeteria.

B Look at the list in Exercise 1A again. Write questions for these answers. Pay attention to the underlined words. Then listen and check.

1. **Q:** *What's Amy going to do?*
   A: She's going to <u>set up the snack table</u>.

2. **Q:** _____
   A: <u>Josh</u> is going to serve the pizza.

3. **Q:** _____
   A: They're going to sign the card <u>in the classroom</u>.

4. **Q:** _____
   A: She's going to <u>wrap the gift</u>.

5. **Q:** _____
   A: They're going to have the party <u>on Friday from 3 to 5 p.m.</u>

3. Speaking

Imagine a party you would like to have. Think about people to invite, the location, the day, and the food. Answer your classmates' questions.

Classmate 1 Where are you going to have the party?
You I'm going to have it at my house.
Classmate 2 When are you going to have it?
You Next Saturday.
Classmate 3 Who are you going to invite?
You I'm going to invite . . .

Special Events 75

Lessons 21 & 22 Mini-review

1. Language check

A Look at the pictures. Then write sentences.

1. (Doug / wrap a gift)

Doug isn't going to wrap a gift. He's going to write a letter.

2. (Jenna / walk her dog)

3. (John and Ali / wash their father's car)

4. (Susan and Carol / do their homework)

5. (Ms. Johnson / wash the windows)

6. (Kyle and Betti / have a bake sale)

B Write questions about tomorrow. Then answer them with your own information.

1. **Q:** (do homework) *Are you going to do homework tomorrow?*
   A:

2. **Q:** (play soccer)
   A:

3. **Q:** (walk a dog)
   A:

4. **Q:** (see a friend)
   A:

C Look at Andrea's calendar. Write questions and answers about her plans for the next week using the correct form of *be going to*.

Monday	Tuesday	Wednesday	Thursday	Friday	Saturday	Sunday
Meet Lynn yoga class — 6:00 p.m.	soccer practice in the park — 4:00	soccer practice — 4:00 babysit — 8:00	soccer practice — 4:00 walk Mrs. Kimball's dog — 6:30	soccer practice — 4:00 meet John — 7:00 at the movie theater	yard work for fund-raiser — 9:00 a.m. buy birthday card for Dad	???

1. **Q:** (What time / have yoga class / Monday)
   What time is she going to have yoga class on Monday?
   A: *She's going to have yoga class at 6:00 p.m.*

2. **Q:** (Where / have soccer practice / Tuesday) _____
   A: _____

3. **Q:** (When / walk / Mrs. Kimball's dog) _____
   A: _____

4. **Q:** (Who / meet / movie theater) _____
   A: _____

5. **Q:** (What time / do yard work / Saturday) _____
   A: _____

6. **Q:** (What / buy / for her dad) _____
   A: _____

2. Listening

T.86 Deanna and Mandy make plans for next week. Check (✓) the best answer to each question.

1. What's Deanna going to do on Monday?
   ☑ go to the library   ☐ go to the gym
2. When's she going to give her presentation?
   ☐ on Monday   ☐ on Wednesday
3. Who's she going to meet on Thursday?
   ☐ Steve   ☐ Sherri
4. Where's she going to go on Friday?
   ☐ to a movie   ☐ to yoga class
5. When are they going to go to the mall?
   ☐ on Saturday   ☐ on Sunday

Time for a Game?
See page 119.

Special Events

Lesson 23

Dance clothes

1. Word power

A What are they wearing? Complete the sentences with the words in the box. Then listen and practice.

☐ checked	☐ flowered	☐ polka-dot	☑ striped
☐ denim	☐ plaid	☐ solid	☐ tie-dyed

1. He's wearing _striped_ socks.
2. She's wearing a _____ skirt.
3. He's wearing _____ pants.
4. She's wearing a _____ hat.
5. He's wearing a _____ jacket.
6. She's wearing a _____ T-shirt.
7. He's wearing a _____ tie.
8. She's wearing a _____ dress.

B Which clothes in Part A are casual? Which clothes are formal? Complete the chart.

Casual clothes	Formal clothes
the striped socks	the solid skirt

C Tell a classmate your opinions of the clothes in Part A.

> I really like the denim jacket. I don't like . . .

Unit 6

2. Language focus

A Olivia and Eddie are talking at the dance. Listen and practice.

Olivia I'm nervous. I don't know anybody here. How can you be so relaxed?
Eddie Well, I know some of the people here. I know Tom . . .
Olivia Which one is Tom?
Eddie He's the one in the checked shirt.
Olivia Oh, I see him. He's cute.
Eddie And I know the Patten sisters, and . . .
Olivia Whoa! Slow down. Which ones are the Patten sisters?
Eddie They're the ones in the tie-dyed T-shirts. Do you want me to introduce you?
Olivia Sure. But introduce me to Tom first!
Eddie OK. Come on. Let's catch him right now.

Which one / Which ones . . . ?

Which one is Tom?
He's **the one** in the checked shirt.
Which ones are the Patten sisters?
They're **the ones** in the tie-dyed T-shirts.

B Look at the picture. Write questions and answers about the people. Then listen and check.

Mark   Nate   Paul   Brenda   Anna   Rene

1. (Mark) **Q:** *Which one is Mark?*
   A: *He's the one in the tie-dyed T-shirt.*
2. (Nate) **Q:** _____
   A: _____
3. (Paul) **Q:** _____
   A: _____
4. (Brenda) **Q:** _____
   A: _____
5. (Anna and Rene) **Q:** _____
   A: _____

Special Events 79

Lesson 24: After the dance

1. Language focus

A Amy and Felipe clean up after the dance. Listen and practice.

Amy Hi, Felipe. What are you doing?
Felipe I'm looking for my CDs. I brought five to the dance.
Amy Let's look over there by the snack table.
Felipe OK. Hey! Whose denim jacket is this?
Amy It's Andrea's. I guess she forgot it. And look! Whose CDs are these?
Felipe They're mine. But there were two more.
Amy Well, maybe someone took them by mistake. Let's go and check at the Lost and Found tomorrow.
Felipe OK. I hope we find them. Those are my favorite CDs.

Whose...?
Whose denim jacket is this?
It's **Andrea's**.

Possessive pronouns
Whose CDs are these?
They're **mine / his / hers / yours / theirs / ours**.

B Look at the items at the Lost and Found. Whose are they? Write questions and answers. Then listen and check.

1. Andrea
2. Josh
3. Sarah
4. Mandy
5. Jenna
6. Andy

1. **Q:** Whose hat is this?
   A: It's Andrea's.
2. **Q:** _____
   A: _____
3. **Q:** _____
   A: _____
4. **Q:** _____
   A: _____
5. **Q:** _____
   A: _____
6. **Q:** _____
   A: _____

C Read the sentences and use the words in the box to write sentences with the same meaning. Then listen and check.

☐ hers ☐ his ☑ mine ☐ ours ☐ theirs ☐ yours

1. It's my backpack.   *It's mine.*
2. It's your cell phone.   _____
3. They're his CDs.   _____
4. It's her wallet.   _____
5. They're our books.   _____
6. They're their magazines. _____

2. Word power

A Look at the other things students left in the room after the dance. What should the students do with them? Write the items in the correct columns.

☑ cell phone   ☐ digital camera   ☐ paper tablecloth   ☐ serving forks
☐ chairs   ☐ dirty paper decorations   ☐ plaid sweater   ☐ two tickets to the dance
☐ clean paper cups ☐ dirty paper plates   ☐ punch bowls   ☐ wallet

Put away	Throw away	Take to the Lost and Found
		cell phone

B Talk to a classmate about what the students should do with the items.

What should they do with the cell phone?   They should take it to the Lost and Found.

3. Listening

People are waiting for their rides home. Listen and match the people to the correct cars.

☐ Amy   ☐ Andrea   ☐ Luigi   ☑ Mandy   ☐ Mr. Garcia

1. *Mandy*
2. _____
3. _____
4. _____
5. _____

Special Events

UNIT 6 Get Connected

Read

A Read the e-mail quickly. Check (✓) the fund-raiser activities you find.

- ☐ clean up the school
- ☐ eat breakfast
- ☐ present a play
- ☐ donate money
- ☐ have a recycling contest
- ☐ sell snacks

Go-Green Club Fund-raiser

Hi, Jimmy!

I have some exciting news. I joined the Go-Green Club at school last week, and it's a lot of fun! We help to clean up the school, and we also help the neighborhood recycling programs.

We're going to hold the East High Go-Green Fund-raiser next Saturday in the school gym. It's going to start at 9:00 a.m. Can you come? We're going to **donate** the money to the town's **recycling center**.

At the fund-raiser we're going to have a recycling contest, so please bring your **used** cell phones, **computer ink cartridges**, and old clothes. The person who brings the most items wins a T-shirt. We're also going to present a play – *Don't Trash It, Reuse It!* The actors are all Go-Green Club members, and I'm one of the actors. Tickets are $15 each. And we're also going to sell a lot of delicious **organic** snacks, so don't eat breakfast!

Please tell your family and friends about the fund-raiser. We want to raise a lot of money.

Hope to see you there!
Kimberly

More Vocabulary Practice? See page 124.

B 🎧 T.94 Read the e-mail slowly. Check your answers in Part A.

C Answer the questions.

1. Who's going to hold a fund-raiser?
   The East High Go-Green Club is going to hold a fund-raiser.
2. When's it going to start? _____
3. Are they going to donate the money to the school? _____
4. What are they going to present? _____
5. What are they going to sell? _____

We're going to . . .

Listen

A 🎧 T.95 Ryan and Elsa talk about a clean-up project. Listen and answer the questions.

1. What's the Go-Green Club going to clean up?
   They're going to clean up the park behind the school.
2. Who's Ryan going to take to a piano lesson? _____
3. What time is the clean up going to start? _____
4. Is Ryan going to help Elsa? _____
5. What are they going to do after the cleanup? _____

B What do you think? Write *I agree* or *I disagree*. Give reasons.

1. Student clubs are a good idea. _____
2. It's important to donate money to good programs. _____
3. Fund-raisers are a good idea. _____
4. It's important to recycle. _____

Your turn

Write

A Imagine you're a member of a new club. You're going to plan a fund-raiser or a club project. Answer the questions.

1. What kind of club is it? _____
2. What's the name of your club? _____
3. What kind of fund-raiser or project are you going to have? _____
4. When and where is it? _____
5. Why are you going to have it? _____

B Write an e-mail to a friend about your fund-raiser or club project. Use the answers in Part A to help you.

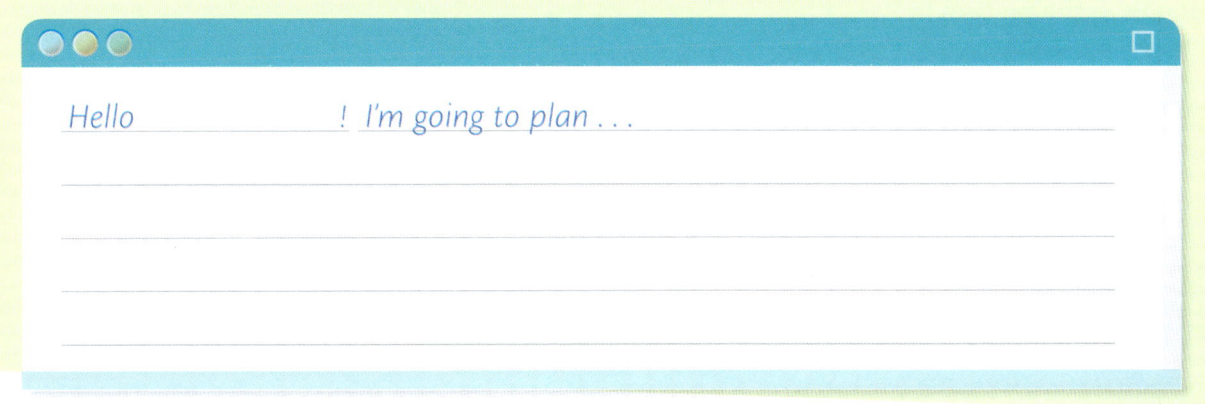

Hello _____ ! I'm going to plan . . .

Special Events

UNIT 6 Review

Language chart review

be going to
I**'m going to** use the Internet.
Are you **going to** do your homework?
Yes, I am.
Is Buster **going to** take the bus?
No, he isn't.

Wh- questions with *be going to*
Who's going to walk the dogs?
Kat **is going to** walk the dogs. / Kat **is**. / Kat.
What's Art **going to** write about?
He**'s going to** write about Ronaldo.
Ronaldo.

A Look at the picture. Then write *Yes / No* questions with *be going to* and answer them.

1. (Teddy / read a book)

    Q: *Is Teddy going to read a book?*

    A: *No, he isn't. He's going to play music.*

2. (Melanie and Georgia / serve the sandwiches)

    Q: _____

    A: _____

3. (Bethany / wrap gifts)

    Q: _____

    A: _____

B Look at the picture in Part A again. Then write questions and answers. Pay attention to the underlined words.

1. **Q:** *Where are they going to have the party?*

    A: They're going to have the party <u>in the cafeteria</u>.

2. **Q:** _____

    A: Melanie and Georgia are going to serve <u>the sandwiches</u>.

3. **Q:** Who's going to pour the drinks?

    A: _____

Language chart review

Which one / Which ones . . . ?
Which one is Matt?
He's **the one** with the guitar.

Whose . . . ?
Whose notebook is this?
It's **Mary's / hers**.

Possessive pronouns
It's **mine / his / hers / yours / theirs / ours**.

C Look at the picture. Then write questions and answers.

Darren   **Min**    **Lenny**    **Jill and Wendy**

1. **Q:** (Darren) _Which one is Darren?_   **A:** _He's the one with the guitar._
2. **Q:** (Min) _____   **A:** _____
3. **Q:** (Lenny) _____   **A:** _____
4. **Q:** (Jill and Wendy) _____   **A:** _____

D Look at the pictures below and the information in Part C. Write questions. Then complete the answers with possessive pronouns.

1. **Q:** _Whose sandwich is this?_
   A: It's _his_ .
2. **Q:** _____
   A: They're _____ .
3. **Q:** _____
   A: It's _____ .
4. **Q:** _____
   A: They're _____ .

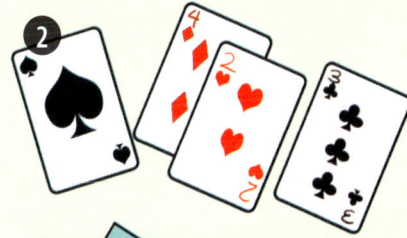

Take another look!

Circle the correct answer.

1. We _____ use a form of the verb *be* in sentences and questions with *going to*.
   a. always   b. sometimes   c. never
2. Which word or phrase best completes this question: "_____ pink sneakers are these?"
   a. Who is   b. Who's   c. Whose

Time for the Theme Project?
See page 131.

Special Events 85

Lesson 25: The blackout

1. Language focus

A Felipe and Mandy share stories about the blackout last night. Listen and practice.

> **Past continuous statements**
> I **was watching** TV with my family.
> We **were riding** the elevator.
> We **weren't moving**.

Felipe Hey, Mandy! Did the electricity go out at your house last night?

Mandy Yeah. It went out at about 8:30. I was watching TV with my family. We were watching my favorite show. Was there a blackout in your neighborhood, too?

Felipe Yes! I had a terrible experience. I was going home with my sister. We were riding the elevator up to our apartment. There were no other people in the elevator. Suddenly, it stopped. There wasn't any light. We weren't moving. We were really scared.

Mandy How awful! Were you in the elevator for a long time?

Felipe No, only about five minutes, but it seemed like five hours! It was so dark!

B What were these students doing at 8:30? Complete the sentences with the past continuous. Then listen and check.

1. **Annie** At 8:30, my sister and I _were watching_ (watch) a basketball game in the gym. Our school team _____ (play) really well, and we _____ (win). Then the lights went out, and the game stopped. We were very disappointed.

2. **Kevin** I was at a concert. The band _____ (play) my favorite song, "Love and Tears." I _____ (not dance), but I was singing with the band. Everybody _____ (have) a great time. Then the lights went out, and the music stopped!

3. **Shanya** My friends and I were at an amusement park. We _____ (have) fun. We _____ (not think) about our school or homework! We _____ (ride) the roller coaster, and we _____ (scream). Suddenly, the ride stopped. We began to scream even louder!

2. Listening

A What were Amy, Josh, Luigi, and Andrea doing at 8:30? Listen and write the correct name under each photo.

_T.98_

_____   _____   _____   _____

B Where were they at the time of the blackout? Listen again. Then write the places.

_T.99_

1. Amy: _in her room_
2. Josh: _____
3. Luigi: _____
4. Andrea: _____

3. Pronunciation Contrastive stress

A Listen. Notice the change in the meaning of a sentence when different words are stressed. Then listen again and practice.

_T.100_

> **Q:** Was your **brother** riding the elevator?
> **A:** No, my **sister** was riding the elevator.

> **Q:** Was your brother **riding the elevator**?
> **A:** No, he was **walking up the stairs**.

B Circle the words you think will be stressed. Then listen and check.

_T.101_

1. **Q:** Were you and your mother watching a movie at home?
   A: No, we were watching a TV show.

2. **Q:** Were you and your mother watching a movie at home?
   A: No, we were watching a movie at the movie theater.

4. Speaking

Ask your classmates what they were doing at these times. Complete the chart. Then share your information with the class.

What were you doing . . . ?	Classmate	Activity
1. an hour ago		
2. at 6:00 this morning		
3. at 9:00 last night		
4. yesterday at noon		

> Billy was eating lunch an hour ago.

Our Stories 87

Lesson 26: Scary experiences

1. Language focus

A Study the chart. Ted went white-water rafting last summer. Look at the pictures and number the sentences in the correct order. Then listen and check.

Past continuous vs. simple past (*when*)		
Action in progress		**Completed action**
We **were talking**	**when**	the water **got** rough.
I **was heading** toward some rocks	**when**	I **saw** the branch.

Note: The completed action can begin the sentence.
When the water **got** rough, we **were eating** lunch.
My friends **found** me **when** I **was resting** under a tree.

____ When the water got rough, we were eating.
_1_ We were having a great time. It was a beautiful day.
____ My friends found me when I was resting under the tree and trying to get dry.
____ I was reaching for an oar when a big wave hit our raft. I fell into the river.
____ I was heading toward some rocks when I saw the branch of a big tree in front of me. I grabbed the branch and held onto it.

B Complete these sentences about scary experiences. Use one verb in the simple past and one in the past continuous. Then listen and check.

1. A bad storm _started_ (start) when I _was walking_ (walk) home from school yesterday.
2. We _____ (cook) hot dogs over our campfire when a bear _____ (come) into our camp!
3. I _____ (read) in bed late last night when someone _____ (knock) on the door.
4. My sister and I _____ (visit) the zoo when a lion _____ (escape) from its cage!
5. When the big dog _____ (jump) on him, Paulo _____ (go) to the mall.
6. Jessica _____ (fly) home from vacation last summer when suddenly the plane _____ (drop) 1,000 feet.
7. I _____ (watch) a horror movie on TV when my cat _____ (jump) out the window.
8. When the tree _____ (fall) on our house, I _____ (study).

C Write sentences about scary experiences. Use the past continuous and the simple past. Then listen and check.

1. (eat dinner / strange man / come to the door)
   I was eating dinner when a strange man came to the door.
   OR _When I was eating dinner, a strange man came to the door._

2. (read in bed / lights / go out)

3. (talk on the phone / hear someone scream)

4. (walk to school / man / grab my bag)

5. (watch TV / storm / hit)

2. Listening

People are describing scary experiences. Listen and check (✓) what happened.

1. ☐ They heard a noise.
   ☐ They made a noise.
2. ☐ It began to rain.
   ☐ It began to snow.
3. ☐ She was lost.
   ☐ She lost her backpack.
4. ☐ His board broke.
   ☐ He fell into the water.

Lessons 25 & 26 Mini-review

1. Language check

A Last night was Jodi's first night at camp. What were the campers doing at 6:00?

1. (Jodi) *She was setting up the tent.*
2. (Adrienne) _____
3. (Bill and Kate) _____
4. (Mr. O'Day) _____
5. (Ricardo) _____

B Complete Jodi's diary entries about camp. Use the simple past or the past continuous.

Monday 8:30 p.m.
The sun **was shining** (shine) when we **arrived** (arrive) today. But it _____ (get) cloudy in the afternoon. We _____ (make) our campfire when it _____ (start) to rain. The fire went out, so we ate cold hot dogs in our tents. Yuck!

Wednesday 9:00 p.m.
Yesterday was OK. We _____ (have) a great morning today, but trouble started in the afternoon. I _____ (sit) at a picnic table when a large branch from a big tree _____ (fall) on my tent.

I was frustrated, but I guess I was lucky! Later, I _____ (set up) my tent again when a bear _____ (come) into our campsite. Mr. O'Day _____ (talk) on the phone. The bear _____ (eat) our hot dogs, and it _____ (look) in our bags! Finally, it _____ (leave).

Friday 4:30 p.m.
I _____ (sleep) all day yesterday. Today is my last day at camp. I'm going home tomorrow, and I'm glad!

Unit 7

C Choose the correct ending for each sentence.

1. I was watching TV when _____
   - ☑ my parents came home.
   - ☐ my parents were coming home.
2. When the bell rang, _____
   - ☐ Mr. Ito gave us homework.
   - ☐ Mr. Ito was giving us homework.
3. Carla and Dan were washing the windows when _____
   - ☐ it started to rain.
   - ☐ it's starting to rain.
4. I was swimming _____
   - ☐ when the water's getting rough.
   - ☐ when the water got rough.
5. When my dog barked, _____
   - ☐ Julian was knocking on my door.
   - ☐ Julian is knocking on my door.
6. When the lights went out, _____
   - ☐ we played a video game.
   - ☐ we were playing a video game.

2. Listening

A Jack sent text messages to four friends. Listen and check (✓) what each person was doing when Jack sent the text messages.

	Playing a video game	Walking home	Cooking dinner	Shopping
1. Tina		✓		
2. Sophia				
3. Mark				
4. Leo				

B Write sentences for each item in Part A.

1. *Tina was walking home when Jack sent her a text message.*
   OR *When Jack sent Tina a text message, she was walking home.*
2. _____
   OR _____
3. _____
   OR _____
4. _____
   OR _____

Time for a Game?
See page 120.

Lesson 27: Close calls

1. Language focus

A A talk-show host interviews a teen who survived an avalanche. Listen and practice.

Host So, David, you survived the biggest avalanche in ten years! We're glad that you're here.
David Thanks.
Host I'd like to ask you some questions. First, what were you doing on Cannon Mountain?
David We were skiing on the north side of the mountain. It has the best snow.
Host Was it snowing that day?
David No, it wasn't. Actually, it was very sunny.
Host Who were you skiing with?
David I was skiing with my family – my parents and my sister.
Host Were many other people skiing?
David No. We were the only ones.

Past continuous questions

Yes / No questions

Was it **snowing**?
Yes, it was.
No, it wasn't.
Were other people **skiing**?
Yes, they were.
No, they weren't.

Wh- questions

What were you **doing**?
We were skiing.
Who were you **skiing** with?
I was skiing with my family.
My family.

B Complete the interview questions. Then listen and check.

Host What _were_ you _doing_ (do) when the avalanche hit?
David My father and I were climbing up the trail.
Host _____ you _____ (carry) your skis?
David Yes, we were.
Host Where _____ your mother and sister _____ (walk)?
David They were walking behind us, lower down the trail. They saw the avalanche first and started shouting.
Host What _____ they _____ (shout)?
David They were shouting, "Go right! Go right!" I looked, and I saw the snow coming down the mountain.
Host _____ it _____ (come) down the mountain very quickly?
David Yes, it was. It was coming really fast. We moved to the right – just in time.

92 Unit 7

C Marilyn was on a frozen lake last winter when the ice cracked. A talk-show host is asking her questions. Read her answers and write his questions. Then listen and check.

1. **Q:** (What) *What were you doing on the lake?*
   A: I was skating on it.

2. **Q:** (Were)
   A: No, I wasn't skating alone.

3. **Q:** (Who)
   A: I was skating with my friend, Sarah. My father and brother were near the lake, too.

4. **Q:** (What)
   A: They were throwing snowballs at each other.

5. **Q:** (Was)
   A: No, it wasn't snowing, but it was really cold.

6. **Q:** (Where)
   A: Sarah was skating on the other side of the lake. But she saw me fall in, and she screamed loudly. My father found a rope and pulled me out. I'm lucky to be alive!

2. Speaking

Imagine a bad experience. Use an idea from the box or your own idea. Your classmates ask questions about it, using the past continuous.

You	I broke my arm.
Classmate 1	What were you doing when you broke it?
You	I was playing basketball.
Classmate 2	Were you shooting the ball?
You	No. I was running.
Classmate 3	Where were you playing?
You	I was playing in the gym.
Classmate 4	Who were you playing with?
You	Trish and Carmen.

The electricity went out.

I broke my arm.

A bad storm hit my town.

My computer crashed.

I broke my leg.

A woman on a bicycle ran into me.

Our Stories 93

Lesson 28: Sharing stories

1. Word power

A Read the students' opinions of these books. Then listen and practice.
T.110

Name: Josh
Title: The Lost Picture
Type of book: Mystery

The book really keeps your attention. Who has the missing painting? I don't think you can guess. You have to read to the *surprising* end.

Name: Andrea
Title: The Wild Side of the Garden
Type of book: Fantasy

The author creates an *unusual* world. Cars fly, and dogs talk. Everyone is reading this *delightful* book. Get it from the school library.

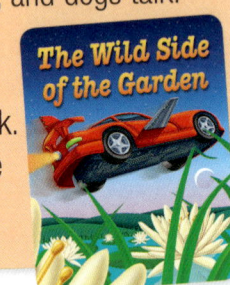

Name: Felipe
Title: The House in Space
Type of book: Science fiction

The book is about a family on Jupiter. It's very *confusing*. There are too many characters. You don't know who is who. Don't even start this book. It's very *disappointing*.

Name: Amy
Title: Hit the Top 10
Type of book: Nonfiction

The book has great information about the music business. It's a really *informative* book. You're going to like it a lot.

Name: Luigi
Title: Alone in the Wild
Type of book: Adventure

A boy is lost in the woods. How is he going to survive? What danger is he going to face? The book is very *suspenseful*!

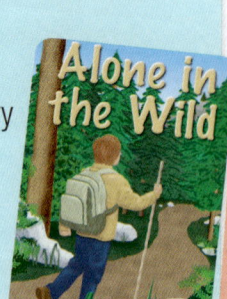

Name: Mandy
Title: Sarah at School
Type of book: Realistic fiction

The book is *dull*. It has too much information on Sarah's family. I wanted to know more about Sarah. There are better books about teens.

B Tell your partner the types of books you like and don't like. Use the adjectives from Part A to explain why.

> I like mystery books. They're surprising. I don't like . . .

94 Unit 7

2. Language focus

A Mandy wrote a book report about *Blind Flight*. Listen and practice.

Past continuous vs. simple past (*while*)	
Action in progress	**Completed action**
While they **were flying**,	a bird **hit** the windshield.

Note: The completed action can begin the sentence.
A bird **hit** the windshield **while** they **were flying**.

Name: *Mandy*
Title: *Blind Flight*
Type of book: *Realistic fiction*

This is an amazing story. Thirteen-year-old Debbie Whitfield had to fly and land a plane, but she was blind.

While Debbie and her uncle were flying, a large bird hit the windshield. The glass broke and hurt her uncle. He didn't move.

Debbie turned the radio controls until she heard a pilot. Soon she was flying while he gave her instructions.

While Debbie was flying, two other planes came to help her. They guided her to the airport. Her friends and family were waiting when she and her uncle arrived.

B Read another student's book report about *Arnie and the Flood*. Complete the sentences using *while* and verbs in the simple past or the past continuous. Then listen and check.

_____While_____ Arnie _was driving_ (drive) home, it _____ (start) to rain very hard. Arnie got to a bridge near his house, and he slowly started to cross it. _____ he _____ (cross) the bridge, the water suddenly _____ (get) higher. It reached his car, and it took his car into the river. Luckily, he got out of the car. A woman _____ (see) him _____ he _____ (try) to swim to land. She helped him to safety.

3. Listening

Students are talking about books. How do they describe them? Check (✓) the correct adjectives.

Book 1
- ✓ interesting
- ☐ unusual

Book 2
- ☐ informative
- ☐ dull

Book 3
- ☐ delightful
- ☐ confusing

Book 4
- ☐ dangerous
- ☐ suspenseful

Book 5
- ☐ surprising
- ☐ disappointing

UNIT 7 Get Connected

Read

A Read the article quickly. Check (✓) the true statements.

☐ 1. Some animals help their owners when they are in danger.

☐ 2. Dogs help people, but cats don't.

☐ 3. The people rescued the animals and the animals rescued the people.

Pet Heroes

This story is about two amazing pets, one dog and one cat. Both are **heroes**. Tank, a three-year-old dog, saved Anna Croft's life. Anna was eating her dinner when she started to **choke**. Tank **pushed** her down to the floor. He jumped up and down on her **chest** until the food came out of her throat. Anna knows that Tank saved her life. She says, "Every time I look at him I think 'You're awesome!'" Lola, a 12-year-old cat, saved her family from dangerous **carbon monoxide**. While Kate and George Lewis were sleeping, Lola came to their bed. Lola **meowed** loudly and pushed her nose into Kate's ear until she **woke up**. Kate tried to tell her husband and daughter to leave the house, but they wouldn't wake up. Kate called 911 for help. They're OK today because Lola saved their lives!

Both owners **rescued** Tank and Lola when they were very young. Years later, both Tank and Lola saved Anna and the Lewis family. That's really incredible!

More Vocabulary Practice? See page 125.

B 🎧 T.114 Read the article slowly. Check your answers in Part A.

C Are these statements true or false? Write *True* or *False*. Then correct the false statements.

1. Anna was eating her dinner when she started to choke.
   True.

2. Tank pushed Anna down to the floor.
   _____

3. While Kate and George were sleeping, Lola meowed loudly.
   _____

4. Kate's husband and daughter woke up easily.
   _____

5. Tank and Lola were rescued when they were old.
   _____

We were hiking when . . .

Listen

A 🎧 T.115 **Kathy and Hiro talk about a camping trip. Listen and answer the questions.**

1. Why is Max amazing? *He saved Hiro's life last summer.*
2. What was Hiro's family doing when he decided to go hiking? _____
3. Was Hiro climbing the biggest rock when he fell? _____
4. Was Max quiet while Hiro was shouting? _____
5. When did Hiro's dad find him? _____

B What do you think? Answer the questions.

1. Do you think pets can be heroes? _____
2. Do you think pets are smart? _____
3. Do you think it's good to go hiking alone? _____
4. Do you think it's important for families to go on vacation together?
_____

Your turn

Write

A Think of an amazing story. Answer the questions.

1. Who / What is it about? _____
2. When did it happen? _____
3. Where did it happen? _____
4. What was the amazing thing about it? _____
5. How does it end? _____

B Write about an amazing story. Use the answers in Part A to help you.

This is an amazing story about . . .

UNIT 7 Review

Language chart review

Past continuous statements
I **was studying** at the library.
She **wasn't eating** cake at the party.

Past continuous questions

Yes / No questions
Were the boys **playing** baseball?
Yes, they were. / No, they weren't.

Wh- questions
What was the baby **doing**?
She was playing.

A Daniel's family was very busy yesterday at 4:00 p.m. Complete the sentences with the affirmative or negative past continuous.

1. Daniel _wasn't reading_ a book.
2. Kathy _____ cards.
3. Mr. Jones _____ TV.
4. Kelly _____ TV.
5. Mrs. Jones _____ a soda.
6. Max and Liam _____ video games.

B Look at the picture and information in Part A. Then complete the questions with *Was*, *Were*, *Who*, or *What* and the correct verb forms.

1. **Q:** _Was_ Mr. Jones _listening_ to music? **A:** No, he wasn't.
2. **Q:** _____ was Mrs. Jones _____ to on the computer? **A:** She was talking to her mother.
3. **Q:** _____ Kathy _____ cards with Daniel? **A:** No, she wasn't.
4. **Q:** _____ Kelly _____ ? **A:** Yes, she was.
5. **Q:** _____ was Daniel _____ ? **A:** He was doing his homework on his computer.
6. **Q:** _____ Max and Liam _____ TV? **A:** No. They were playing video games.

Language chart review

Past continuous vs. Simple past (*when*)
I **was reading** a book **when** the phone **rang**.
When he **came** home, I **was sleeping**.

Past continuous vs. simple past (*while*)
She **listened** to music **while** she **was doing** chores.
While I **was walking** in the park, I **met** an old friend.

C Look at the pictures. Then write sentences with the past continuous + *when* and the simple past.

1. Kelly / sleep / the dog jump on her
   Kelly was sleeping when the dog jumped on her.

2. Daniel / do homework / his phone ring
   _____

3. Kathy / play cards / get hungry
   _____

4. Mrs. Jones / talk on the computer / the power go out
   _____

D Rewrite the sentences in Part C with *while*. Then circle the action in progress and underline the completed action in each sentence.

1. While (Kelly was sleeping,) the dog jumped on her.
2. _____
3. _____
4. _____

Take another look!

Circle the correct answer.

1. In past continuous sentences with *when*, the action in progress goes _____ the completed action of the sentence.
   a. only before   b. only after   c. before or after

2. Verb forms that refer to actions in progress end in _____ .
   a. *-ing*   b. *-ed*   c. *-'s*

Time for the Theme Project?
See page 132.

Our Stories

Lesson 29

How do I get there?

1. Word power

A Look at the map. Complete each sentence with the correct place. Then listen and practice.

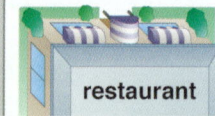

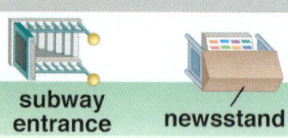

T.116

1. The _grocery store_ is across from the newsstand.
2. The _____ is next to the post office.
3. The _____ is across from Jenny's apartment building.
4. The _____ is between the shoe store and the bakery.
5. The _____ is between the restaurant and the newsstand.
6. The _____ is next to the apartment building.
7. The street vendor is across from the _____ .
8. The _____ is on Orange Street, between Blue and Green Streets.
9. The _____ is behind the apartment building.
10. The souvenir shop is across from the _____ .

B Think of a place in Part A. Can your classmate guess the place?

You It's across from the grocery store.
Classmate Is it the newsstand?
You No, it's not.
Classmate Is it the subway entrance?
You Yes, it is.

2. Language focus

A Jenny lives in the neighborhood in Exercise 1A. Amy calls Jenny to get directions. Listen and practice.

Amy Hi, Jenny. I just got off the subway. How do I get to your apartment?
Jenny Where are you exactly?
Amy I'm on Blue Street, in front of a newsstand.
Jenny OK. Cross the street and turn left. Go straight ahead to the first intersection. There's a flower shop on the corner, on your right.
Amy Uh-huh.
Jenny Turn right on Orange Street, and go straight ahead.
Amy Yeah.
Jenny My apartment building is on the next corner, on your right. To get to the entrance, turn right. It's across from the bakery. Got it?
Amy I think so. I can call you again if I get lost.

Directions
Turn right on Orange Street.
Turn left at the first corner.
Go straight ahead.
Go past the subway entrance.
Cross the street.

Locations
It's **on the corner**.
It's **on the left / on your left**.
It's **on the right / on your right**.
It's **across from** the bakery.

B Complete the directions from Jenny's apartment to the following places. Use the map in Exercise 1A. Then listen and check.

1. **street vendor:** Go outside and turn right. _Go_ to the first corner and _____ the street. Turn _____. Go _____ the café to the first intersection. _____ the street and _____ left. It's _____ from the skyscraper.

2. **souvenir shop:** Go outside and turn left. At the first corner, turn _____ again. Then go straight to the intersection and _____ the street. There's a restaurant on the _____. The souvenir shop is across from the restaurant.

3. Listening

A Listen. Jenny is giving Amy directions from her apartment. Where does Amy want to go? Look at the map in Exercise 1A. Then check (✓) the correct places.

1. ☐ video store ☐ laundromat ☐ health club
2. ☐ flower shop ☐ grocery store ☐ post office
3. ☐ bakery ☐ clothing store ☐ restaurant
4. ☐ subway entrance ☐ laundromat ☐ café

B Give a classmate directions to one of the places Amy didn't go to in Part A. Your classmate says the place.

> Go outside and cross Green Street. Then cross Orange Street. It's on the corner.

> It's the health club.

> Yes.

Lesson 30: Street fair

1. Language focus

A Amy is telling Luigi about her visit with Jenny. Listen and practice.

Luigi Did you have fun with Jenny?
Amy Yeah! We had a great time, especially on Sunday. There was a street fair in her neighborhood.
Luigi What was the fair like? Were there a lot of people? Was there any good food?
Amy It was crowded, but it was fun. The food was *great*! I had grilled chicken and potato salad.
Luigi Was there a raffle?
Amy No. There wasn't a raffle. There weren't any rides, either, but there were some cool things for sale. I bought a necklace and a tie-dyed T-shirt.

There was a / There were some
There wasn't any / There weren't any

There was a street fair.
There were some cool things for sale.
There wasn't a raffle.
There wasn't any ice cream.
There weren't any rides.

Was there a / Were there any . . . ?

Was there a raffle?
Yes, there was. / No, there wasn't.
Was there any good food?
Yes, there was. / No, there wasn't.
Were there any rides?
Yes, there were. / No, there weren't.

B Complete the sentences about the fair. Then listen and check.

1. *There wasn't any* jewelry.
2. _____ street vendors.
3. _____ skateboarders.
4. _____ drawings.
5. _____ artist.
6. _____ sports equipment.
7. _____ band.
8. _____ children's clothes.
9. _____ newsstand.

102 Unit 8

C What did Amy see at the fair? Write questions, and look again at the picture on page 102 to answer them. Then listen and check.

1. (a hot-dog stand) **Q:** *Was there a hot-dog stand?* **A:** *Yes, there was.*
2. (rides) **Q:** _____ **A:** _____
3. (music) **Q:** _____ **A:** _____
4. (books for sale) **Q:** _____ **A:** _____
5. (dogs) **Q:** _____ **A:** _____
6. (a police officer) **Q:** _____ **A:** _____
7. (flowers) **Q:** _____ **A:** _____

2. Pronunciation Stress

A Listen. Notice how *was* and *wasn't* are generally unstressed in questions and affirmative statements but stressed in short answers. Then listen again and practice.

Unstressed	Stressed
Q: Was there a street fair yesterday?	A: Yes, there **was**.
Q: Was there any country music?	A: No, there **wasn't**.

There was a great band.
There was a table with clothes for sale.

B Practice the questions and answers in Exercise 1C in pairs. Focus on the stress.

3. Speaking

A Complete the survey questions with *Was there* or *Were there*.

B Complete the survey for yourself. Then ask a classmate the questions.

Event survey		You		Classmate	
		Yes	No	Yes	No
1. *Was there* any good food?		☐	☐	☐	☐
2. _____ any music?		☐	☐	☐	☐
3. _____ any cool things to buy?		☐	☐	☐	☐
4. _____ any games?		☐	☐	☐	☐
5. _____ any rides?		☐	☐	☐	☐
6. _____ a lot of people?		☐	☐	☐	☐

C Tell the class about your classmate's event in Part B.

> Tim went to a carnival last summer. There were great rides! There weren't any . . .

Lessons 29 & 30 Mini-review

1. Language check

A Complete the sentences with *a*, *an*, *any*, or *some*.

1. There wasn't ____any____ pizza at the fair.
2. There were _____ good singers at the concert.
3. There were _____ potato chips at the hot-dog stand.
4. There wasn't _____ artist at the street fair.
5. There weren't _____ jeans in the store.
6. There was _____ band at my school last week.
7. There wasn't _____ ice cream at the party.
8. There was _____ raffle at the school festival.

B Look at the picture. Then complete the questions and write the answers about the amusement park.

1. **Q:** _Were there any_ roller coasters? **A:** _Yes, there were._
2. **Q:** _____ ice cream? **A:** _____
3. **Q:** _____ concert? **A:** _____
4. **Q:** _____ hot-dog stands? **A:** _____
5. **Q:** _____ dogs? **A:** _____
6. **Q:** _____ police officer? **A:** _____
7. **Q:** _____ lot of people? **A:** _____
8. **Q:** _____ fun house? **A:** _____

C Lucy is having a party. Her friends are calling to get directions to her house. Complete the conversations.

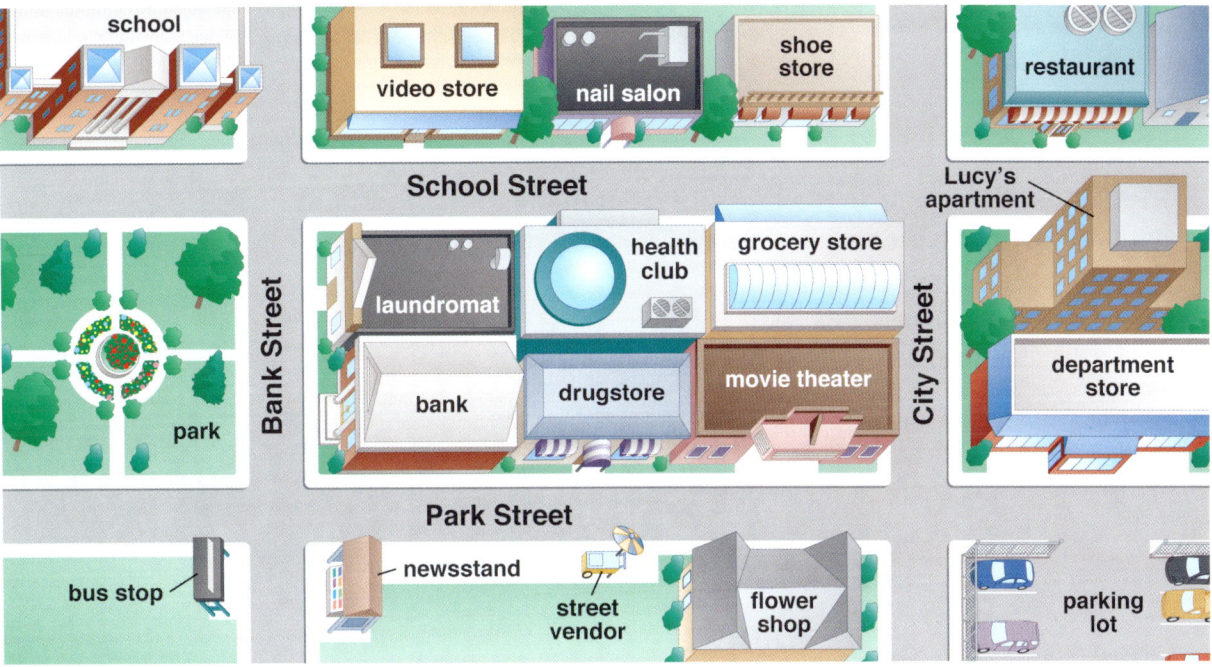

1. **Marta** Hi, Lucy? It's Marta. I'm lost.
   Lucy Where are you?
   Marta I'm on Bank Street. I'm in front of the laundromat and _across from_ the park. I'm looking at the park.
   Lucy Oh, you're close. Walk to the _____ of Bank and School Streets. Then _____ on School Street. _____ the health club. After the health club, there's a grocery store on the corner. _____ City Street and _____. My apartment entrance is on your _____.

2. **Jake** Hi, Lucy? It's Jake. How do I get to your apartment?
   Lucy Hi, Jake. Where are you?
   Jake I'm _____ of Park Street and Bank Street in front of the bus stop. I'm looking at the newsstand.
   Lucy OK. Cross Bank Street and _____ on Park Street. _____ to the next intersection. _____ City Street and turn left. _____ Park Street and _____ to School Street. _____, and you'll see my apartment on your _____. It's _____ the restaurant.

2. Listening

Five friends came to Lucy's house early to help. She sent them to buy things for the party. Listen and follow her directions on the map in Exercise 1C. Where did each friend go? Number the places.

☐ flower shop   ☐ grocery store   ☐ video store

_1_ street vendor   ☐ drugstore

Time for a Game? See page 121.

Lesson 31: Things to do

1. Word power

A Read about the events in New York City. Complete the suggestions with the correct sentences in the box. Then listen and practice.

- ☐ Go people-watching.
- ☐ Take a helicopter ride.
- ☑ Try public transportation.
- ☐ Go window-shopping.
- ☐ Try an ethnic restaurant.
- ☐ Visit a famous landmark.

6 things to do in New York City

1. *Try public transportation.*
   Take a subway and then a ferry to Staten Island. Enjoy a great view of the Statue of Liberty.

2. Go to Queens.
   _____
   Eat dishes from India, Greece, or Colombia.

3. _____
   This is the most expensive way to see the city, but the view from the sky is amazing.

4. _____
   The Empire State Building is one of the most popular sights in the city.

5. _____
   Everyone visits Times Square. There are always lots of people, and it's never dull.

6. See the latest fashions on Fifth Avenue. No money? No problem. _____
   You don't have to buy – you can just look!

B Which three things would you most like to do in New York City? Why? Tell a classmate.

> I'd like to go to Queens. I'd like to try an ethnic restaurant. I'd also like to . . .

2. Language focus

Why don't we / We could for suggestions
Why don't we take the ferry?
We could take the subway.

I'd rather for preferences
I'd rather go to Little Italy.

A Lisa is visiting her friend Kate in New York. Listen and practice.

Kate Are there any special things you want to do in New York?
Lisa Yes. I want to see the Statue of Liberty. Why don't we take the Staten Island Ferry?
Kate OK. That's a fun thing to do. Then let's try an ethnic restaurant. You know, public transportation here is great. We could take the subway to Chinatown.
Lisa Actually, I'd rather go to Little Italy. I really want some pizza.
Kate Oh, you *always* want pizza.
Lisa Well, I'm not going to change just because I'm in New York!

B Complete Kate's suggestions and Lisa's preferences. Then listen and check.

1. **Kate** (take a ferry) We _could take a ferry_ .
   Lisa (take a helicopter ride) _I'd rather take a helicopter ride._

2. **Kate** (take the subway) Why _____?
   Lisa (walk) _____

3. **Kate** (go to a museum) We _____.
   Lisa (see a play) _____

4. **Kate** (go window-shopping) Why _____?
   Lisa (go people-watching) _____

5. **Kate** (try an Indian restaurant) We _____.
   Lisa (try Greek food) _____

3. Speaking

Imagine your classmate is a visitor to your city or town. Write names of places to go. Then make suggestions to a classmate.

1. a store _____
2. an ethnic restaurant _____
3. a good view _____
4. a museum _____
5. a landmark _____
6. a park _____

Why don't we go to Haru Sushi?

I'd rather go to a concert at the high school.

In the City

Lesson 32: We didn't go . . .

1. Language focus

A Martin is on a class trip to Boston. Read his e-mail to his friend Larry. Then listen and practice.

> Tuesday, May 16
>
> Hi, Larry!
>
> We're having a great time, and we're seeing all the sights. We visited two famous landmarks – Paul Revere's House and the John F. Kennedy National Historic Site. Yesterday we went to Faneuil Hall Marketplace because we wanted to shop. It was great! I bought lots of souvenirs. Today, we went to Boston Common – a big park. We didn't stay long because the weather was bad. We're going to go again tomorrow. See you soon.
>
> Martin

Clauses with *because*

We went to Faneuil Hall Marketplace **because we wanted to shop**.

We didn't stay long **because the weather was bad**.

B What else did Martin do or not do on Tuesday? Why or why not? Complete the sentences with *because* + the reasons in the box. Then listen and check.

- ☐ he couldn't get tickets
- ☐ he wanted to see a special exhibit
- ☑ it rained
- ☐ he wanted Chinese food
- ☐ he wanted to shop
- ☐ public transportation was faster

1. He didn't take a walking tour *because it rained*.

2. He went to Chinatown _____.

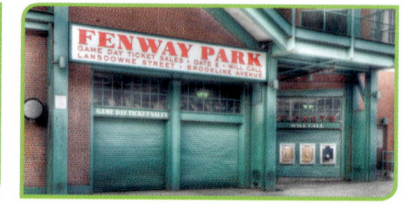

3. He didn't see a baseball game _____.

4. He didn't take taxis _____.

5. He went to the museum _____.

6. He went to the stores on Newbury Street _____.

108   Unit 8

C Martin and his group went back to their hotel on Tuesday night. Complete the sentences with the simple past. Use the negative when necessary. Then listen and check.

1. Martin and his friends ___walked___ (walk) back to their hotel because there were no taxis.
2. The kids ___didn't take___ (take) a walk after dinner because it was raining.
3. The kids _____ (eat) dinner in a fast-food restaurant near the hotel because it was cheap.
4. Val and Ollie _____ (get) stamps because the hotel shop was closed.
5. Steve _____ (call) home because he promised to call his parents every day.
6. Penny _____ (buy) the T-shirt because it was too expensive.
7. Greg _____ (write) postcards because he forgot.
8. Bailey _____ (write) in her diary because she didn't want to forget about her trip.
9. Martin _____ (watch) the news on TV because he wanted to know about the weather for the next day.
10. The kids _____ (go) to bed early because they had to wake up at 6:00 a.m.

2. Listening

Martin met a new friend, Carla, in the lobby of his hotel. Did Carla do the things in the chart? Listen and check (✓) the things she did.

1. ☐ She went to Boston Common.
2. ☐ She walked the Freedom Trail.
3. ☐ She went to a science museum.
4. ☐ She went to a classical concert.
5. ☐ She went to a rock concert.

3. Speaking

A Look at the chart. Check (✓) the things you *didn't* do last weekend. Then write three more things you *didn't* do.

☐ call a friend   ☐ do homework   ☐ go to the beach
☐ clean my room   ☐ go shopping   ☐ go to the movies

B Now tell the class about the things you didn't do. Give reasons.

> I didn't go to the movies because there weren't any new ones.

In the City 109

UNIT 8 Get Connected

Read

A Read the article quickly. Answer the question.

What's a famous landmark you can see? _____

Old San Juan

A walking tour of Old San Juan is the best way to see the beautiful, **historic** houses, museums, and shops. The streets can get crowded, but you can stop and rest at one of the delightful outdoor cafés.

First, go to the Plaza Colón. There is a famous landmark in the **plaza** – a statue of Christopher Columbus. He came to America in 1492.

Walk past the beautiful Tapia Theater to the **harbor**. Visitors can enjoy drama and dance at the theater. At the harbor, you can see giant **cruise ships**. There's a beautiful, old post office near the harbor. In front of the post office, there's a small **tourist information office**. You can get maps and other information there.

And don't forget to see the **forts** in San Juan, including La Fortaleza, a famous fort built in 1553. It's a **national historic site**. Do you want to see skyscrapers, too? Then you have to leave Old San Juan. Read on . . .

More Vocabulary Practice? See page 125.

B T.132 Read the article slowly. Check your answer in Part A.

C Answer the questions.

1. Where's the statue of Christopher Columbus? *It's in the Plaza Colón.*
2. Where can visitors enjoy drama and dance? _____
3. What's in front of the post office? _____
4. What can you get there? _____
5. What's the name of a very famous fort? _____

Why don't you go there!

Listen

A T.133 Julie and Andreas talk about San Diego. Listen and write *True* or *False*. Then correct the false statements.

1. ~~Julie~~ Andreas went to San Diego two summers ago. *False*
2. Everyone in Andreas's family likes to do the same things. _____
3. Julie doesn't like shopping. _____
4. There are 13 museums near the park. _____
5. Andreas thinks the most interesting place in San Diego is the zoo. _____

B What do you think? Write *I agree* or *I disagree*. Give reasons.

1. It's a good idea to try new things. _____
2. It's important to travel to learn about different cultures. _____
3. Visiting museums is an interesting way to learn about a country's culture.
   _____
4. Shopping isn't good to do on a vacation. _____

Your turn

Write

A Write a suggestion for a place to go on vacation. Then write four suggestions of things you can do there. Use *Why don't you* or *You could*.

Why don't you go to _____ (place)

1. _____
2. _____
3. _____
4. _____

B Write an e-mail to your friend about a place to go on vacation. Use the answers in Part A to help you.

Hi, _____ ! I have a great suggestion for a place to go on vacation. Why don't you go to . . .

In the City

UNIT 8 Review

Language chart review

Directions
Turn left at the second corner.
Go past the grocery store.

Locations
The flower shop is on the corner.
The bakery is on the left / on your left.

Clauses with *because*
We went to the bakery because we wanted to buy some bread.
I didn't buy the dress because it was too expensive.

A Stacy is asking her grandmother how to get to different places in town. Look at the map. Then circle the correct phrases to complete the conversations.

1. **Stacy** How do I get to the flower shop?
   Grandmother (**Go past** / Keep going) the bakery. Cross Center Street.
   (Turn right / Turn left) and cross Park Street.
   It's (across the street / on your right).

2. **Stacy** How do I get to the restaurant?
   Grandmother (Go straight on / Cross) Park Street. Cross Center Street. It's
   (on the right / on the left), across from the parking lot.

3. **Stacy** How do I get to the post office?
   Grandmother (Cross / Go straight on) Park Street. Cross Center Street. Then
   (turn left / turn right). The entrance is (on your left / on your right).

B Write sentences about Stacy. Use the simple past and *because*.

1. go / flower shop / want to buy flowers
   Stacy went to the flower shop because she wanted to buy flowers.

2. go / bakery / be hungry

3. go / post office / want to send some letters

4. not go / restaurant / be closed

5. not go / park / be cold

Language chart review

Why don't we / We could for suggestions
Why don't we go to the movies?
We could go to the movies.

Was there a / Were there any . . . ?
Were there any good restaurants?
Yes, there were. / No, there weren't.

I'd rather for preferences
I'd rather go to a museum.

There was a / There were some / There wasn't any / There weren't any
There was an Italian restaurant. / There weren't any cafés.

C Stacy's grandmother is making suggestions, and Stacy is expressing preferences. Complete the conversations with the verb phrases in the box.

- ☑ eat Chinese food / Mexican food
- ☐ take the subway / ferry
- ☐ try the cake / ice cream

1. **Grandmother** _Why don't we eat Chinese food?_ OR _We could eat Chinese food._
   Stacy I don't like Chinese food. _I'd rather eat Mexican food._
2. **Grandmother** _____
   Stacy I don't like the subway. _____
3. **Grandmother** _____
   Stacy It's too sweet. _____

D Complete Stacy's e-mail to her friend. Use *there was, there were, there wasn't, there weren't,* and *were there*.

Hi, Kira,
I'm having a wonderful time visiting my grandmother. We visited a small town yesterday. There were a lot of fun things to do there. _There were_ great clothing stores. I didn't buy any jewelry, because _____ any interesting jewelry stores. _____ a cheap music store, so I didn't buy any new CDs. _____ any good restaurants? Yes, _____. My grandmother and I ate at a cool Mexican place. I tried some delicious cookies, too. _____ an awesome bakery in town.
Stacy

Take another look!

1. Which sentence is a suggestion? Circle the correct answer.

   a. We'd rather eat pizza.   b. We shouldn't eat pizza.   c. We could eat pizza.

2. Write the suggestion in number 1 another way.

Time for the Theme Project? See page 133.

UNIT 1 Game *Memory game*

Look at the picture for two minutes. Then write six more questions about the picture on a separate piece of paper. Close your book. Take turns asking a classmate your questions. Who remembers the most?

What are Lenny and Ellie doing?

Who plays tennis?

What color is Chuck's T-shirt?

UNIT 2 Game *My trip to France*

Play the game with a classmate. Use things in your bag as game markers.
Use a coin to find out how many spaces to move. Heads = 1, Tails = 2.
Rules:
- Take turns. Flip a coin and move your marker to the correct space.
- Look at the picture. Make sentences about what you did on your trip using the verb phrases in the box.

    Classmate 1 *I flew to Paris.*
    Classmate 2 *That's correct!*
    ▶ No mistakes? Stay on that space.
    ◀ Mistakes? Move back one space.
- The person who gets to FINISH first, wins.

☐ drink French coffee
☐ eat French bread
☐ fly to Paris
☐ make some friends on the plane
☐ practice French
☐ rent inline skates
☐ see the Eiffel Tower
☐ shop for souvenirs
☐ sleep in a hotel
☐ take a boat ride
☐ take many pictures
☐ try French food in a restaurant
☐ visit the museum
☐ walk around the city
☐ write postcards

UNIT 3 Game *How would you feel?*

A Imagine you do each thing below. How would you feel? Circle the answers so they are true for you.

1. You spend ten hours at a theme park.
   a. You're exhausted.
   b. You're glad.
   c. You're frustrated.

2. You go on a city tour of New York City.
   a. You're relaxed.
   b. You're worried.
   c. You're excited.

3. You go to a summer camp for a month.
   a. You're homesick.
   b. You're worried.
   c. You're glad.

4. Your friends give you a surprise birthday party.
   a. You're embarrassed.
   b. You're surprised.
   c. You're relaxed.

5. You spend a week at a ski resort.
   a. You're excited.
   b. You're exhausted.
   c. You're worried.

B Circle the points below for your answers in Part A.

Question	Answer *a*	Answer *b*	Answer *c*
1	2 points	3 points	1 point
2	2 points	1 point	3 points
3	2 points	1 point	3 points
4	1 point	3 points	2 points
5	3 points	2 points	1 point

Add the points for your answers: _____ How much fun do you have?

11 – 15 points   You have a lot of fun. You enjoy everything.
 6 – 10 points   You have fun, but sometimes you worry.
 1 – 5 points   You have a little fun, but you worry a lot.

C Work with a classmate. Compare your answers in Part A.

You You spend ten hours at a theme park. You're . . .
Classmate . . . Well, I'm exhausted. And you?
You I'm glad.

D Walk around the classroom. How many people have the same score as you? _____

UNIT 4 Game *Comparison race*

Kyle and Lydia have the same birthday, but their families are different. How? Work with a classmate. Write seven more sentences comparing people. The pair that finishes first is the winner.

Kyle's father is taller than Lydia's father.

1. _____
2. _____
3. _____
4. _____
5. _____
6. _____
7. _____

thin   relaxed
athletic   active
   old
short
   tall

Unit 4 Game   117

UNIT 5 Game Crossword puzzle

Read the clues and write your answers in the puzzle.

Across
1. Try warm chicken soup when you have this.
4. When you have this, it's difficult to talk.
6. Your elbows are part of these.
7. Your knees are part of these.
8. You have these on your feet.
9. You use this to talk and eat.

Down
1. You have these on your hands.
2. This is below your head.
3. When they have this, many people use eardrops.
5. Many people take aspirin when they have this.
8. You have one of these on each hand.

UNIT 6 Game *Big plans*

Play the game with a classmate. Use things in your bag as game markers.
Use a coin to find out how many spaces to move. Heads = 1, Tails = 2.
Rules:
- Take turns. Flip a coin and move your marker to the correct space.
- Answer the question or follow the directions.
    Classmate 1 *I'm go to walk my dog after school.*
    Classmate 2 *That's a mistake! It's "I'm going to."* Move back 1 space.
    ▶ No mistakes? Stay on that space.
    ◀ Mistakes? Move back one space.
- On a "free space," ask a classmate any question. Keep your marker on that space until your next turn.
- The person who gets to FINISH first, wins.

START

- What are you going to do after school?
- Are you going to buy anything this weekend? If yes, what?
- Who are you going to eat dinner with tonight?
- Ask a classmate about his or her plans for tonight.

- Ask a classmate what time he or she is going to bed tonight.
- **Free Space** — Ask a classmate a question.
- When are you going to do today's homework?
- Are you going to do yard work this year?
- **Free Space** — Ask a classmate a question.

- Where are you going to do your homework?
- How many hours are you going to watch TV tonight?
- Are you going to see any movies this month? If yes, name them.
- Are you going to have a test this week? If yes, in what class?
- Ask a classmate if he or she is going to study tonight.

FINISH

- Are you going to go to a party or a special event next month? If yes, what?
- Is your school going to have a fund-raiser this year? If so, when?
- Are you going to clean your room this week?
- Ask a classmate if his or her mother or father is going to do any chores this weekend.

UNIT 7 Game What was happening...?

Play with a classmate.

Classmate 1 Look at Picture 1 for one minute. What was everyone doing when the rain started? Close your book and write as many things as you can remember in two minutes.

Classmate 2 Look at Picture 2 for one minute. What was everyone doing when the rain stopped? Close your book and write as many things as you can remember in two minutes.

Tell your classmate what you wrote. Check each other's information. Who remembered the most?

Picture 1: When the rain started

Picture 2: When the rain stopped

Nicki was water-skiing when the rain started.

Yes. One point!

120   Unit 7 Game

UNIT 8 Game *What's missing?*

A Look at the map of the town center. It's almost empty now, but it wasn't ten years ago. Imagine what was in the town center. Label six buildings with words from the box.

| supermarket | restaurant | flower shop | gas station | skating rink |
| apartment building | movie theater | drugstore | shoe store | department store |

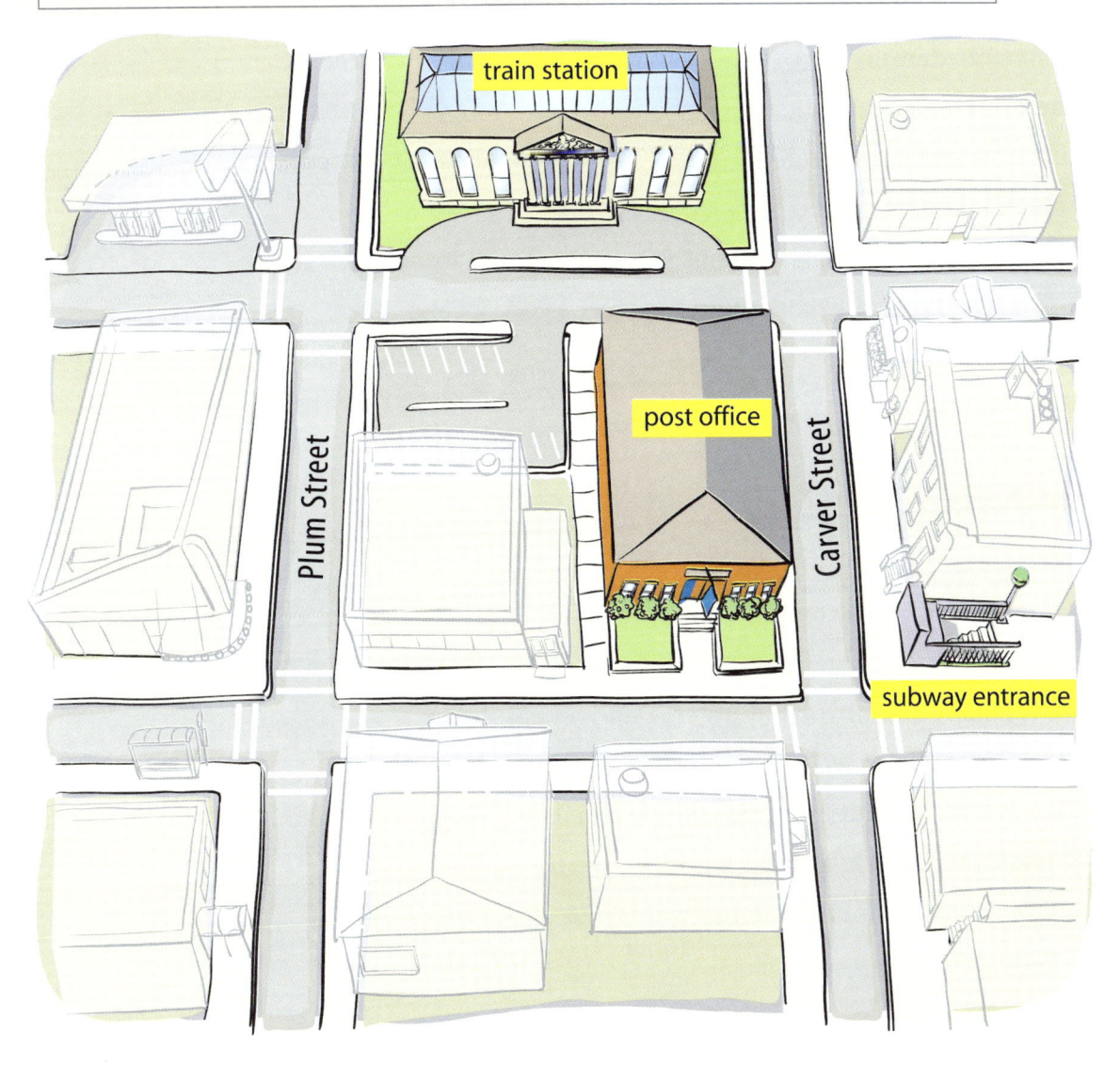

(Map labels: train station, post office, Plum Street, Carver Street, subway entrance)

B Work with a classmate.

Classmate 1   Guess what places are on Classmate 2's map. Ask *Was there* and *Were there* questions.

Classmate 2   Guess what places are on Classmate 1's map. Ask *Was there* and *Were there* questions.

- Was there a restaurant?
- Yes, there was.
- Were there any flower shops?
- No, there weren't.

Who can identify all of the places with the fewest guesses?

Get Connected Vocabulary Practice

UNIT 1

The underlined words belong in other sentences. Write the words where they belong.

1. It's difficult to <u>waters (n.)</u> a sailboat in bad weather. _navigate_
2. My science teacher makes <u>overcoming fear (v. phrase)</u> fun to learn. _____
3. My little brother hates dogs. He's <u>row (v.)</u> them. _____
4. Would you like to try a <u>afraid of (adj.)</u>? They're delicious! _____
5. Let's take a boat trip on the city's <u>ecology (n.)</u>. _____
6. <u>Navigate (v.)</u> of the water is difficult for some people learning to swim. _____
7. My friends and I <u>crab (n.)</u> a boat on the river every weekend. _____

UNIT 2

Circle the correct words to complete the sentences.

1. Some people work hard to save (amazing / **endangered**) species in Africa.
2. That's a (giant / beautiful) hamburger! Can you eat it all?
3. Giant (persons / tortoises) can live over 200 years.
4. (Islands / Marine iguanas) eat vegetables and aren't dangerous at all.
5. Before we (flew / snorkeled) in the water, we took a few lessons.
6. A (sea lion / Galapagos) lives in the water and eats a lot of fish.
7. The (scientist / scenery) on this island is so beautiful and green!

UNIT 3

Match the words to the meanings.

1. skills (n.) __g__
2. modern (adj.) ____
3. miles (n.) ____
4. ended (v.) ____
5. journey (n.) ____
6. scary (adj.) ____
7. diplomat (n.) ____

a. stopped
b. trip
c. frightening
d. one of these is 1,609 meters
e. new; popular now
f. a person who represents a country
g. the ability to do something well

UNIT 4

Complete the sentences with the words in the box.

| ☐ miles per hour (n.) | ☐ opened (v.) | ☑ outdoor (adj.) | ☐ rides (n.) | ☐ traveled (v.) |

1. We don't swim in our pool in the winter. It's an ____outdoor____ pool and it's too cold.
2. The bus _____ very slowly. It took one hour to go from my house to school.
3. Some race horses can run 40 _____ .
4. A lot of teens think the _____ at amusement parks are exciting.
5. A Mexican restaurant _____ last month in my neighborhood.

Get Connected Vocabulary Practice

UNIT 5

What words mean the same as the underlined words? Circle the correct answers.

1. Christina's <u>self-esteem (n.)</u> grew when she got an A on her history report.
    a. health   (b.) good feelings about herself
2. My <u>philosophy (n.)</u> of life is to be a good friend.
    a. what someone believes is a good way to live life   b. a way to reduce stress
3. With more practice and <u>discipline (n.)</u>, Kayla has a good chance to win the singing contest.
    a. control   b. doing something in a flexible way
4. Regular exercise is a good <u>benefit (n.)</u> for your health.
    a. helpful thing   b. relaxing thing
5. Vincent studies <u>martial arts (n.)</u> three times a week.
    a. ways to create art   b. sports that teach self-defense
6. Joe has the flu so he <u>probably (adv.)</u> can't go to school tomorrow.
    a. he's pretty sure he   b. he's especially sad he
7. Mrs. Torres teaches a class on <u>self-defense (n.)</u> at the community center.
    a. challenging yourself   b. protecting yourself

UNIT 6

Complete the advertisement with the words in the box.

☐ computer ink cartridges (n.)   ☐ donate (v.)   ☐ organic (adj.)   ☑ recycling center (n.)   ☐ used (adj.)

Come to Centerville's _recycling center_ for a fund-raiser this Saturday afternoon between 1:00 and 3:00. We're going to have contests, games, and lots of information on recycling. We're going to sell _____ fruits and vegetables from local farmers. Bring your _____ cell phones, bottles, cans, and newspapers to recycle. Also, bring your old _____ and get a free black one! We're going to _____ all the money to build a new and better recycling center. Come and help our planet!

124 Get Connected Vocabulary Practice

UNIT 7

Circle the correct words to complete the sentences.

1. My sisters (jumped up / (woke up)) very early Saturday morning.
2. He couldn't move because a big branch fell across his (owner / chest).
3. My uncle (rescued / started) a little girl from the rough water.
4. A lot of young kids (choke / save) on small toys.
5. I think the teens who saved the baby's life are (owners / heroes).
6. (Carbon monoxide / Throat) is very dangerous.
7. The cat (meowed / pushed) until we gave her some milk.
8. Look! That boy (smiled / pushed) that girl on the bike. That wasn't nice!

UNIT 8

Circle the correct answers.

1. Lewis and Clark made _____ journey.
   a. a new (adj.)   (b.) an historic (adj.)
2. There was a festival in the town _____ .
   a. flower shop (n.)   b. plaza (n.)
3. There are a lot of boats in the _____ .
   a. street (n.)   b. harbor (n.)
4. We took a two-week vacation on a big _____ .
   a. cruise ship (n.)   b. canoe (n.)
5. Let's get maps at the _____ .
   a. tourist information office (n.)   b. post office (n.)
6. That country has really strong _____ . No one can easily come into the country.
   a. forts (n.)   b. cruise ships (n.)
7. The Statue of Liberty in New York City is a _____ .
   a. skyscraper (n.)   b. national historic site (n.)

UNIT 1

Theme Project: Make a brochure for a field trip.
Theme: Citizenship
Goal: To learn more about rules for visiting a place in your community

At Home

Read the rules for a farm field trip.

Good Food Farm is a popular place for school field trips. Students can learn about farm animals and about growing food there. They can also enjoy time outdoors. Here are some rules students have to follow at the farm:
Students . . .
1. have to stay in small groups and stay with the guide.
2. have to bring their own lunch.
3. can touch some of the animals, but they have to ask the guide first.
4. can't feed the animals.

Where would you like to go on a field trip? What rules would there be on the trip? Complete the chart. Use your dictionary, if necessary.

Place:
Rule 1 _____
Rule 2 _____
Rule 3 _____
Rule 4 _____

Draw pictures or bring photos to class of where you would like to go on a field trip.

In Class

- **Look at all of the field trips and the rules. Choose one field trip.**

- **Make a brochure. Use the sample brochure as a model.**

- **Choose a group leader. Present your brochure to another group.**

  > We'd like to visit the City Art Museum. You have to bring money for lunch. You have to . . .

- **Display the brochures in your classroom. Walk around and look at all of them. Which field trip would you like to go on?**

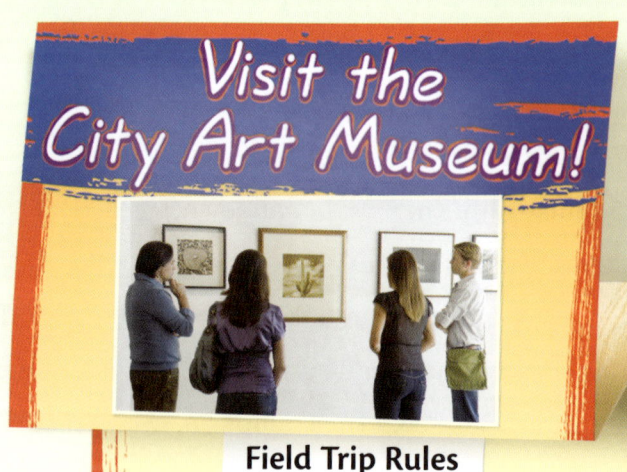

Visit the City Art Museum!

Field Trip Rules

You have to . . .
· bring money for lunch.
· turn off your phone in the museum.

You can't . . .
· bring big bags into the museum.
· take photos.

Sample brochure

UNIT 2

Theme Project: Make a group photo album.
Theme: Diversity; citizenship
Goal: To learn about events that are special to your classmates

At Home

Read about school vacation activities.

> What did students around the world do on their last school vacation? Some students took care of their younger brothers or sisters. Others worked, attended school classes, or went to camps, like theater camps, music camps, or sports camps. Some teens volunteered in their community, and they did not get paid. Some students stayed home and relaxed or studied. And, of course, many students took trips with their families.

Write four things you did on vacation. Use your dictionary, if necessary.

1. _____   3. _____
2. _____   4. _____

Draw pictures or bring photos of the things you did on vacation to class.

In Class

- **Make a photo album page of your vacation. Use the sample album page as a model.**

- **Tell your group about your vacation.**

  > I went with my family to Porto Alegre. We visited the Cultural Center. We went to . . .

- **Make a group photo album. Make a cover for your photo album. Then staple together all of your pages and the cover to make your album.**

- **Display the photo albums in your classroom. Walk around and look at all of them. How many students took trips on their last vacation?**

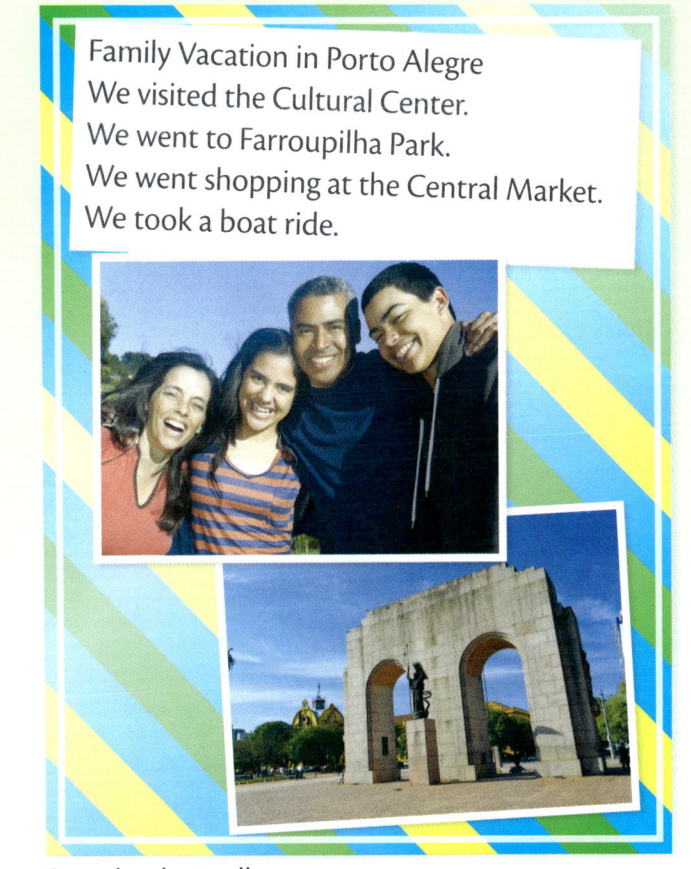

Family Vacation in Porto Alegre
We visited the Cultural Center.
We went to Farroupilha Park.
We went shopping at the Central Market.
We took a boat ride.

Sample photo album page

UNIT 3

Theme Project: Make a bookmark about an interesting person.
Theme: Citizenship; diversity
Goal: To learn more about interesting people

At Home

Read about an interesting person.

Annie Taylor, a teacher, was born in Michigan in the United States in 1838. She wanted to be famous. One day, in 1901, Annie went over Horseshoe Falls in a barrel. (Horseshoe Falls is part of Niagara Falls. It's about 170 feet or 52 meters high.) Annie was 63 when she went over Horseshoe Falls. She was very brave. After she went over the falls, she spoke to many people about this experience, and became famous. She died 20 years later in 1921 at the age of 83.

Choose a person who did something amazing. Answer the questions. Use your dictionary or the Internet, if necessary.

Name: _____
Where was he / she born? (city and / or country) _____
What was his / her special accomplishment? _____
When was his / her special accomplishment? _____
Why do you think this person is interesting? _____

Draw pictures or bring photos of the person to class.

In Class

- **Make a bookmark. Use the sample bookmark as a model.**
- **Present your bookmark to your group.**

> Bruce Lee was born in San Francisco in 1940. He was a famous Chinese American martial arts expert and actor. He . . .

- **Display all the bookmarks in your classroom. Walk around and look at all of them. Which person do you admire the most?**

BRUCE LEE

- He was born in San Francisco in 1940.
- He was a famous Chinese American martial arts expert and actor.
- He started acting, and soon he was a star. He was in **Enter the Dragon**, but he died before the movie opened.

Sample bookmark

UNIT 4

Theme Project: Make fact cards.
Theme: Cultural diversity
Goal: To learn facts about places, people, and things around the world

At Home

Read about how to find out new facts.

- The highest waterfall in the world is Angel Falls in Venezuela.
- The largest island in the world is Greenland.
- The continent of Europe is smaller than the continent of South America.
- The Andes Mountains are taller than the Rocky Mountains.

Where can you find this kind of information? Well, you can find many facts like these in an almanac – a book that gives information about travel, music, sports, countries, and other topics. *TIME Almanac with Information Please* is a popular almanac. You can find it in libraries and bookstores. You can also use *infoplease*® online – it's free!

Find two interesting facts. Look in reference books or on the Internet. Write the facts below. Use a dictionary, if necessary.

1. (comparative) Fact: _____
2. (superlative) Fact: _____

Draw pictures or bring photos of the facts to class.

In Class

- Look at all of the facts. Choose six facts.
- Make six fact cards. Use the sample fact card as a model.
- Exchange cards with another group. Read the other group's cards.
- Come back to your group. Tell your group a new fact that you learned.

> The longest wall in the world is in China. It's called the Great Wall of China.

- Display the fact cards in your classroom. Walk around and look at all of them. Vote on the three most interesting facts.

The longest wall in the world is in China. It's called the Great Wall of China.

Great Wall of China

Sample fact card

Unit 4 Theme Project   129

UNIT 5

Theme Project: Make a booklet of home remedies for illnesses.
Theme: Health
Goal: To learn about different ways to get better when you're sick

At Home

Read about things people do when they are sick.

When you get sick, do you take medicine right away or do you try some other things first? Many people use remedies they know from their family or friends for things like colds, earaches, toothaches, insect bites, sunburns, or other problems. Some families use common remedies, like hot tea for a cold or salt and warm water for a sore throat. But others use unusual remedies. For example, some people put oatmeal on their skin when they have a rash. Other people drink vinegar or garlic and orange juice when they have a cold.

Write two sicknesses or health problems. Then ask someone for a remedy for each one. Complete the chart. Use your dictionary, if necessary.

	Sickness or problem	Person	Remedy
1.			
2.			

Draw pictures or bring photos of your two family members or friends to class.

In Class

1. Make a booklet page for one of your remedies. Use the sample booklet page as a model.

2. Tell your group about your remedy.

   When my grandmother has a cold, she drinks garlic tea.

3. Make a group booklet. Make a cover for your booklet. Then staple together all of your pages and the cover to make your booklet.

4. Display the booklets in your classroom. Walk around and look at all of them. What are the most unusual home remedies? Do you want to try them?

Name: Lucas Mendes
My remedy is from my grandmother.

When I have a cold, I drink garlic tea.

Sample booklet page

130   Unit 5 Theme Project

UNIT 6

Theme Project: Make a poster of things to put in a time capsule.
Theme: Citizenship; multiculturalism
Goal: To think of things that would describe life today to people in the future

At Home

Read about what students at Lincoln High School are going to put in a time capsule.

Students at Lincoln High School are going to create a time capsule. They are going to bury the capsule in front of City Hall. Other students are going to open the capsule – in 50 years!

What are the students going to put in the capsule? Anything that shows what life is like right now. Some students are going to put in popular magazines. Some are going to put in current books and DVDs. Other students are going to bring their own photos and videos to put in the capsule. Students are also going to write letters to the students of the future. They are going to describe their daily lives, popular culture, and world events and problems.

Write five things you would like to put in a time capsule. Use your dictionary, if necessary.

1. _____
2. _____
3. _____
4. _____
5. _____

Draw pictures or bring photos of the things to class.

In Class

- **Look at all of the things to put in a time capsule. Choose the six most interesting things.**

- **Make a poster. Use the sample poster as a model.**

- **Choose a group leader. Present your poster to another group.**

  > We are going to put in a photo of a car, a letter, . . .

- **Display the posters in your classroom. Walk around and look at all of them. What are the most interesting things your classmates are going to put in their time capsules?**

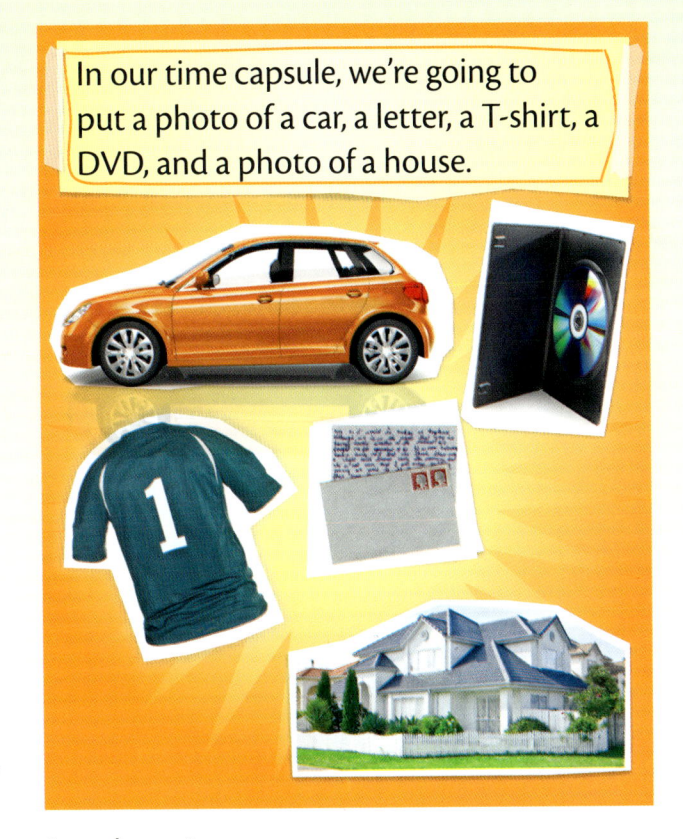

> In our time capsule, we're going to put a photo of a car, a letter, a T-shirt, a DVD, and a photo of a house.

Sample poster

Unit 6 Theme Project   131

UNIT 7

Theme Project: Finish a story to make a book.
Theme: Ethics; citizenship
Goal: To write a story

At Home

Read the story and check (✓) the correct beginning for the first sentence.

_____ when he heard a noise outside in the yard. He sat up in bed and turned on the light. The noise stopped. Mike turned out the light again and tried to go to sleep. After a few minutes, he heard the noise again. Mike called for his father, but his father didn't answer. Mike was afraid. He got up and went downstairs. Mike found the front door open, so he looked outside. He was very surprised when he saw his father in the yard. Mike's father was using Mike's birthday present – a large telescope. He was looking at stars!

☐ 1. Mike isn't really sleeping
☐ 2. When Mike was sleeping
☐ 3. While someone was outside Mike's house
☐ 4. Mike was sleeping in his bed

Write the beginning sentence of a story. Start with **When** and use the past continuous. Use your dictionary, if necessary.

In Class

- Read all of the beginning sentences. Choose one sentence for your story.

- Write the beginning and the middle of the story. Write the end of the story. Draw pictures to illustrate the story. Use the sample book pages as a model.

- Think of a title for your story, and make a cover. Then staple together all of your pages and the cover to make your book.

- Exchange books with another group. Read the other group's book and ask questions about it.

    How old are Ted and Angie?

    They're 20.

- Display the books in your classroom. Walk around and look at all of them. How many stories are similar to yours?

Sample book cover

Ted and Angie were driving in the country late one night when they saw a strange light.

The light was following them! They stopped. The light stopped, too . . .

Sample book pages

132 Unit 7 Theme Project

UNIT 8

Theme Project: Make a map for an ideal neighborhood.
Theme: Citizenship; environment
Goal: To plan and present your ideal neighborhood

At Home

Read about ideal neighborhoods.

> What's an ideal neighborhood like?
>
> Different people have different ideas about what makes an ideal neighborhood. Some people want a neighborhood with everything close to their homes. They want stores, restaurants, a doctor's office, a library, and a playground they can easily walk to.
>
> Others would rather live in a quieter environment. They want a neighborhood they can walk or bicycle in. They also want parks and other places where they can play and walk their dogs and meet other people. They're happy to drive a *little* way to get to the stores, the library, or the doctor's office.

What do you want in your ideal neighborhood? Write four things. Use your dictionary, if necessary.

1. _____   3. _____
2. _____   4. _____

Draw pictures or bring photos of the things to class.

In Class

- Look at all of the things for an ideal neighborhood. Choose eight things.
- Draw a map of your ideal neighborhood. Use the sample map as a model.
- Choose a group leader. Present your map to another group.

> There's a big music store in our neighborhood. It has a lot of cool music. There's a . . .

- Display the maps in your classroom. Walk around and look at all of them. How many maps have the same things?

The Ideal Neighborhood

library | department store
park | electronics store
 | video arcade
school | restaurant
 | music store

Sample map

Verb List

Os verbos estão listados com o número de página do Student's Book em que aparecem pela primeira vez.

Regular Verbs

Present	Past	Page	Present	Past	Page
add	added	64	land	landed	95
agree	agreed	46	learn	learned	10
answer	answered	17	like	liked	2
arrive	arrived	16	listen	listened	2
ask	asked	11	live	lived	39
attend	attended	9	look	looked	11
believe	believed	23	love	loved	2
breathe	breathed	59	meow	meowed	96
brush	brushed	64	miss	missed	8
call	called	17	move	moved	59
camp	camped	37	navigate	navigated	12
care	cared	64	need	needed	4
carry	carried	92	open	opened	10
challenge	challenged	66	organize	organized	73
change	changed	36	perform	performed	10
chat	chatted	8	plan	planned	10
check	checked	24	play	played	2
choke	choked	96	point	pointed	58
clean	cleaned	9	pour	poured	74
cook	cooked	4	practice	practiced	17
crash	crashed	93	prevent	prevented	66
create	created	94	promise	promised	109
cross	crossed	95	protect	protected	66
dance	danced	10	pull	pulled	93
decide	decided	10	push	pushed	96
decorate	decorated	74	race	raced	16
discover	discovered	32	rain	rained	33
donate	donated	82	reach	reached	88
drop	dropped	89	reduce	reduced	66
dry	dried	88	relax	relaxed	59
end	ended	40	remember	remembered	59
enjoy	enjoyed	16	rent	rented	16
escape	escaped	89	rescue	rescued	96
exercise	exercised	11	rest	rested	19
experience	experienced	32	row	rowed	12
face	faced	94	scream	screamed	86
finish	finished	36	seem	seemed	86
floss	flossed	66	serve	served	74
grab	grabbed	88	share	shared	10
guide	guided	95	shine	shined	90
hate	hated	8	shop	shopped	16
head	headed	88	shout	shouted	92
help	helped	59	sign	signed	72
homeschool	homeschooled	13	skate	skated	17
improve	improved	59	skateboard	skateboarded	2
introduce	introduced	79	ski	skied	92
invite	invited	75	skip	skipped	66
join	joined	10	slow	slowed	79
jump	jumped	89	snorkel	snorkeled	16
knock	knocked	89	snow	snowed	89

Present	Past	Page
sound	sounded	11
spill	spilled	42
start	started	11
stay	stayed	9
stop	stopped	16
study	studied	2
survive	survived	92
talk	talked	4
travel	traveled	16
try	tried	16
turn	turned	95

Present	Past	Page
use	used	60
visit	visited	17
wait	waited	17
walk	walked	5
want	wanted	11
wash	washed	64
watch	watched	17
weigh	weighed	50
work	worked	10
wrap	wrapped	74

Irregular Verbs

Present	Past	Page
babysit	babysat	72
be	was	9
become	became	10
begin	began	31
bet	bet	61
break	broke	89
bring	brought	9
build	built	38
buy	bought	5
can	could	4
catch	caught	79
choose	chose	36
come	came	8
cost	cost	52
do	did	23
drink	drank	6
drive	drove	7
eat	ate	5
fall	fell	88
feed	fed	5
feel	felt	39
fight	fought	62
find	found	36
fly	flew	18
forget	forgot	4
get	got	2
give	gave	18
go	went	2
grow	grew	38
hang [out]	hung [out]	2
have	had	2
hear	heard	89
hit	hit	88
hold	held	88

Present	Past	Page
hurt	hurt	59
keep	kept	64
know	knew	36
leave	left	24
lose	lost	89
make	made	4
meet	met	10
overcome [fear]	overcame [fear]	12
put	put	62
read	read	5
ride	rode	5
ring	rang	33
run	ran	65
see	saw	18
send	sent	14
set	set	74
shoot	shot	93
sing	sang	10
sit	sat	7
sleep	slept	18
speak	spoke	31
spend	spent	32
swim	swam	14
take	took	2
teach	taught	13
tell	told	33
think	thought	36
throw	threw	93
wake up	woke up	96
wear	wore	8
will	would	11
win	won	22
write	wrote	11

Word List

Esta lista inclui as palavras e as frases-chave do *Connect Revised Edition* Combo 3. O número que aparece ao lado de cada palavra se refere à página do Student's Book em que elas aparecem pela primeira vez.

Key Vocabulary

Aa
across (37) _____
across from (101) _____
activity (10) _____
add (64) _____
adventure (94) _____
advice (60) _____
afraid of (12) _____
after-school [adjective] (11) _____
ago [two weeks ago] (36) _____
agree (46) _____
ahead (101) _____
airplane (38) _____
airport (95) _____
alive (93) _____
allergies (60) _____
allergy pills (60) _____
alone (10) _____
amusement park (86) _____
ankle (58) _____
another (17) _____
answer [noun] (64) _____
Antarctica (36) _____
anybody (79) _____
anymore (8) _____
anyone (42) _____
anything (23) _____
anyway (33) _____
anywhere (23) _____
apartment building (100) _____
arm (58) _____
arrive (16) _____
artist (102) _____
ask (11) _____
aspirin (60) _____
assistant (38) _____
attend (9) _____
author (94) _____
avalanche (92) _____
aviation [father of . . .] (38) _____
awful (86) _____

Bb
babysit (72) _____
babysitting [noun] (72) _____
back (58) _____
bakery (100) _____
bake sale (72) _____
balloon flight (38) _____
basic (10) _____

be (9) _____
because (107) _____
become (10) _____
bee hummingbird (51) _____
before (59) _____
begin (31) _____
beginner (10) _____
be going to (72) _____
believe (20) _____
bell (33) _____
benefit (68) _____
best (23) _____
best [the best] (92) _____
bet (61) _____
better (64) _____
bike (5) _____
billion (52) _____
blackout (86) _____
blind (95) _____
board (89) _____
body (59) _____
bones (66) _____
born (43) _____
both (52) _____
brain (66) _____
branch (88) _____
break [noun] (33) _____
break [verb] (89) _____
breathe (59) _____
bridge (50) _____
brush [verb] (64) _____
build (38) _____
bumper car (23) _____
bus (8) _____
bus driver (104) _____
by (80) _____

Cc
cabin (20) _____
cage (89) _____
calcium (66) _____
call (17) _____
camp [verb] (37) _____
capital (18) _____
car (28) _____
carbon monoxide (96) _____
care about (64) _____
carefully (59) _____
carnival (103) _____
carry (92) _____

catch (79) _____
cavities (66) _____
Celsius (50) _____
centimeters (50) _____
challenge (66) _____
challenging (46) _____
championship (17) _____
chance [by any chance] (4) _____
change (36) _____
character (94) _____
chat (8) _____
cheap (109) _____
check (24) _____
checked (78) _____
checkup (65) _____
cheetah (51) _____
chess club (10) _____
chess game (10) _____
chest (96) _____
chicken soup (60) _____
Chile (2) _____
chilly (33) _____
choke (96) _____
choose (36) _____
chores (73) _____
city tour (32) _____
class assignment (10) _____
clean [adjective] (81) _____
clean [verb] (9) _____
clearly (59) _____
close call (92) _____
closed (60) _____
cloth (62) _____
clothing store (100) _____
club (10) _____
coastal redwood (51) _____
coffee (52) _____
cold [noun] (60) _____
cold medicine (60) _____
comfortably (59) _____
comparison (44) _____
computer club (10) _____
computer ink cartridge (82) _____
confusing (94) _____
controls (95) _____
corner (101) _____
correctly (59) _____
cost (52) _____
cotton candy (22) _____
could (107) _____

136 Word List

cowboy (20) _____
crab (12) _____
cracker (60) _____
crash (93) _____
crazily (59) _____
create (94) _____
cross (95) _____
cruise ships (110) _____

Dd
dance [adjective] (78) _____
dance [noun] (16) _____
dangers (94) _____
dark (86) _____
decide (10) _____
decorate (74) _____
degrees (50) _____
delicious (46) _____
delightful (94) _____
denim (78) _____
diary (31) _____
did (22) _____
digital camera (81) _____
diplomat (40) _____
dirty (81) _____
disagree (46) _____
disappointed (86) _____
disappointing (94) _____
discipline (68) _____
discover (32) _____
doctor (61) _____
dolphin (56) _____
donate (82) _____
door (89) _____
down (92) _____
drama club (10) _____
drink [noun] (5) _____
drink [verb] (18) _____
drive (7) _____
drop (89) _____
dry (88) _____
dude ranch (32) _____
dull (94) _____
dune buggy (16) _____
dwarf gecko (50) _____

Ee
each other (93) _____
ear (58) _____
earache (60) _____
eardrops (60) _____
eating habits (64) _____
ecology (12) _____
either (72) _____
elbow (58) _____
electricity (86) _____
elephant (46) _____
elevator (86) _____
embarrassed (30) _____
end (40) _____
endangered (26) _____
energy (66) _____

enjoy (14) _____
entertaining (46) _____
entrance (101) _____
escape (89) _____
ethnic restaurant (106) _____
even [adverb] (16) _____
exactly (101) _____
excellent [adjective] (31) _____
exercise [noun] (10) _____
exercise [verb] (11) _____
exhausted (30) _____
expensive (52) _____
experience [noun] (86) _____
experience [verb] (32) _____
exploration (39) _____
explorers (36) _____
eyedrops (60) _____

Ff
face [noun] (58) _____
face [verb] (94) _____
fact (44) _____
fact [in fact] (11) _____
Fahrenheit (50) _____
fall (89) _____
fall in (88) _____
false (19) _____
famous landmark (106) _____
fantasy (94) _____
farewell party (74) _____
fashions (106) _____
fast [adverb] (31) _____
fast-food restaurant (109) _____
fats (66) _____
feed (5) _____
feel (39) _____
feet [measurement] (38) _____
ferry (107) _____
festival (22) _____
fight (62) _____
finally (90) _____
finger (58) _____
finish (36) _____
fireworks (22) _____
flexibly (59) _____
flight (36) _____
flight simulator (28) _____
floss (66) _____
flower (108) _____
flowered (78) _____
flower shop (100) _____
flu (60) _____
foods (64) _____
forts (110) _____
frustrated (30) _____
fund-raiser (73) _____
fun house (22) _____

Gg
garden (94) _____
get (5) _____
get lost (101) _____

get off (101) _____
get ready (5) _____
giant (26) _____
gift (74) _____
giraffe (56) _____
give (18) _____
glad (30) _____
glass (95) _____
gold (18) _____
golf ball (45) _____
go out (24) _____
go past (101) _____
go straight (101) _____
grab (88) _____
grilled chicken (102) _____
grocery store (100) _____
grow [up] (38) _____
guide [noun] (18) _____
guide [verb] (95) _____
guitar player (23) _____
guy [you guys] (44) _____
gym [adjective] (9) _____

Hh
happily (59) _____
harbor (110) _____
hard [adjective] (44) _____
have to (8) _____
head [verb] (88) _____
headache (60) _____
health club (100) _____
health tip (66) _____
hear (89) _____
heel (58) _____
helicopter ride (106) _____
hero (96) _____
hers (80) _____
hey (4) _____
high (50) _____
his (80) _____
historic (110) _____
hit (88) _____
hockey (47) _____
hold (88) _____
homesick (30) _____
homestay (30) _____
hope [verb] (80) _____
horse (33) _____
host family (33) _____
hot-dog stand (103) _____
hotel [adjective] (16) _____
hour (60) _____
How often . . . (64) _____
hurt (59) _____

Ii
important (46) _____
improve (59) _____
inches (50) _____
indoors (67) _____
informative (94) _____
insomnia (62) _____

Word List 137

instruction (95) _____
instructor (59) _____
intersection (101) _____
interview (53) _____
into (93) _____
invite (75) _____

Jj
jeans (104) _____
join (89) _____
journey (40) _____
jump (89) _____
junk food (62) _____

Kk
keep (66) _____
keep up (64) _____
kid (16) _____
kilogram (50) _____
kilometers per hour (56) _____
knock (64) _____

Ll
lake (93) _____
land [noun] (37) _____
land [verb] (95) _____
large (51) _____
laundromat (100) _____
leg (58) _____
lemon (60) _____
level [noun] (10) _____
life (10) _____
light [adjective] (45) _____
light [noun] (86) _____
lion (45) _____
list (74) _____
listener (39) _____
llama (99) _____
local (18) _____
look for (80) _____
loose (59) _____
lose (89) _____
Lost and Found (80) _____
loud (70) _____
loudly (70) _____
lower down (92) _____
luckily (95) _____

Mm
magazine (5) _____
mammal (56) _____
marine iguana (26) _____
marketplace (108) _____
martial arts (68) _____
maté (18) _____
meal (66) _____
meeting (75) _____
member (10) _____
meow (96) _____
meter (50) _____
miles (40) _____
miles per hour (54) _____

mind [noun] (59) _____
mine (80) _____
minerals (66) _____
miss [miss the bus] (8) _____
missing (94) _____
mistake [by mistake] (80) _____
modern (40) _____
moon (28) _____
more than (52) _____
most (52) _____
mountain climbing (36) _____
mountain range (51) _____
mouth (58) _____
move (59) _____
movements (59) _____
music business (94) _____
music video (25) _____
mystery (94) _____

Nn
nail salon (100) _____
national historic site (110) _____
navigate (12) _____
neck (58) _____
nervous (79) _____
news (109) _____
nickname (3) _____
noise (89) _____
nonfiction (94) _____
no one (17) _____
north (92) _____
North America (37) _____
nose (58) _____

Oo
oar (88) _____
often (4) _____
olive oil (62) _____
once (64) _____
one [the one] (79) _____
on foot (37) _____
on the corner (101) _____
on the left / right (101) _____
onto (88) _____
on your left / right (101) _____
open (54) _____
opinion (46) _____
orange juice (61) _____
organic (82) _____
organize (73) _____
ours (80) _____
outdoor (54) _____
outside (101) _____
overcoming fear (12) _____
over there (80) _____

Pp
painting (94) _____
paper cup (81) _____
paper decorations (81) _____
paper plate (81) _____
paper tablecloth (81) _____

part (23) _____
past (101) _____
patiently (59) _____
peacefully (59) _____
people-watching [go . . .] (106) _____
perform (10) _____
philosophy (68) _____
phone call (25) _____
plaid (78) _____
plan [verb] (10) _____
plane (31) _____
planet (50) _____
planetarium (28) _____
play [noun] (11) _____
plaza (110) _____
poem (10) _____
points (44) _____
police officer (103) _____
polka-dot (78) _____
poor (38) _____
populous (52) _____
pose [noun] (59) _____
postcard (18) _____
post office (100) _____
potato salad (102) _____
pour (74) _____
president (11) _____
prevent (66) _____
prize (22) _____
probably (68) _____
program [noun] (10) _____
project (36) _____
promise (109) _____
protect (66) _____
public transportation (106) _____
pull (93) _____
punch [noun] (75) _____
punch bowl (81) _____
push (96) _____
pyramid (51) _____

Qq
quickly (59) _____
quietly (59) _____
quiz (39) _____

Rr
race (16) _____
raffle ticket (22) _____
rain (33) _____
ranch (20) _____
reach (88) _____
reader (39) _____
realistic fiction (94) _____
recycling center (82) _____
reduce (66) _____
regularly (59) _____
relaxed (30) _____
relaxing (46) _____
remember (59) _____
rent (16) _____
reptile (50) _____

rescue (96) _____
rest (19) _____
ride [noun] (22) _____
right [direction] (92) _____
right after (75) _____
ring [verb] (33) _____
rock (88) _____
rodeo (20) _____
roller coaster (46) _____
rope (93) _____
rough (88) _____
row (12) _____
ruins (18) _____

Ss
sadly (59) _____
safari (32) _____
safe (62) _____
safety (95) _____
sale [for sale] (102) _____
salsa [music] (2) _____
samba (16) _____
sawshark (56) _____
scared (86) _____
scary (40) _____
scenery (26) _____
school [adjective] (4) _____
school trip (31) _____
science fiction (94) _____
scream (86) _____
sea horse (56) _____
sea lion (26) _____
seconds [time] (38) _____
seem (86) _____
self-defense (68) _____
self-esteem (68) _____
serve (74) _____
serving fork (81) _____
set [all set] (75) _____
set up (74) _____
share (10) _____
shine (90) _____
shoot [a ball] (93) _____
shop [noun] (16) _____
shop [verb] (108) _____
should (67) _____
shoulders (62) _____
shout (92) _____
side (92) _____
sights (106) _____
sign [verb] (74) _____
sign up (72) _____
skill (40) _____
skin (66) _____
skip (66) _____
ski resort (32) _____
skis [noun] (92) _____
sky (106) _____
skyscraper (100) _____
sleep [noun] (64) _____
slow down (79) _____

slowly (59) _____
snacks (75) _____
snack table (74) _____
snack time (66) _____
snorkel (16) _____
snow [noun] (45) _____
snow [verb] (89) _____
snowballs (93) _____
soccer club (10) _____
soccer practice (15) _____
solar system (28) _____
solid (78) _____
someone (80) _____
sore throat (60) _____
souvenir shop (100) _____
space (75) _____
spaghetti (46) _____
speech (74) _____
speedboat (45) _____
spill (42) _____
spot (16) _____
square kilometers (50) _____
square miles (50) _____
stairs (87) _____
stay away (66) _____
stomach (58) _____
storm (89) _____
story (10) _____
strange (62) _____
strawberry [adjective] (47) _____
street fair (102) _____
street vendor (100) _____
stress (66) _____
stretch (70) _____
striped (78) _____
strong (59) _____
student council (10) _____
stuffed animal (23) _____
subway (101) _____
subway entrance (100) _____
suddenly (86) _____
summer (18) _____
sun (44) _____
sunglasses (80) _____
surfing [noun] (46) _____
surprised (30) _____
surprising (94) _____
survive (92) _____
suspenseful (94) _____
sweets (64) _____

Tt
table (5) _____
take care of (64) _____
taxi (109) _____
tea (18) _____
tears (86) _____
teen [adjective] (66) _____
teen club (32) _____
teeth (64) _____
tent (90) _____

terrible (29) _____
terrific (33) _____
test [noun] (67) _____
than (44) _____
theirs (80) _____
theme park (32) _____
thoughts (10) _____
thumb (58) _____
ticket (28) _____
tie-dyed (78) _____
time [in time] (92) _____
times [three times a day] (64) _____
toe (58) _____
ton (50) _____
too [too exhausted] (31) _____
top (94) _____
topic (36) _____
tortoise (26) _____
tour (18) _____
tour boat (32) _____
tourist information office (110) _____
toward (88) _____
train (8) _____
travel (54) _____
tree (51) _____
trick (20) _____
trivia (50) _____
trouble (90) _____
true (19) _____
try (16) _____
turn [noun] (44) _____
turn [verb] (95) _____
turn left / right (101) _____
twice (64) _____

Uu
uncomfortable (63) _____
unhappy (63) _____
unusual (94) _____
used (82) _____
useful (46) _____

Vv
vegetable (64) _____
video store (100) _____
view (107) _____
vitamins (66) _____
volcano (51) _____
volleyball club (11) _____

Ww
wake up (96) _____
walk dogs (5) _____
wallet (81) _____
was (31) _____
wash (64) _____
waters (12) _____
wave [noun] (88) _____
way (59) _____
way [all the way] (19) _____
Web page (11) _____
weigh (50) _____

welcome (10) _____
well [adverb] (31) _____
were (31) _____
whale (32) _____
What fun! (16) _____
which one(s) (79) _____
white shark (53) _____
white-water rafting (32) _____
whose (80) _____
why (36) _____
Why don't we . . . ? (107) _____
wild (32) _____

win (22) _____
window (72) _____
window-shopping [go . . .] (106) ___
windshield (93) _____
woods (94) _____
work [noun] (6) _____
world record (50) _____
worried (30) _____
would like to (11) _____
would rather [I'd rather] (107) _____
wrap (74) _____
wrist (58) _____

Yy
yard work (72) _____
yesterday (20) _____
yet (67) _____
yoga [noun] (59) _____
yoga class (58) _____
yours (80) _____
yourself (67) _____

Acknowledgments

Connect, Revised Edition has benefited from extensive development research. The authors and publishers would like to extend their particular thanks to all the CUP editorial, production, and marketing staff, as well as the following reviewers and consultants for their valuable insights and suggestions:

Focus Groups

São Paulo Suzi T. Almeida, Colégio Rio Branco; **Andreia C. Alves**, Colégio Guilherme de Almeida; **Patricia Del Valle**, Colégio I. L. Peretz; **Elaine Elia**, Centro de Educação Caminho Aberto; **Rosemilda L. Falletti**, Colégio Pio XII; **Amy Foot Gomes**, Instituto D. Placidina; **Lilian I. Leventhal**, Colégio I. L. Peretz; **Adriana Pellegrino**, Colégio Santo Agostinho; **Maria de Fátima Sanchez**, Colégio Salesiano Sta. Teresinha; **Regina C. B. Saponara**, Colégio N. S. do Sion; **Neuza C. Senna**, Colégio Henri Wallon; **Camila Toniolo Silva**, Colégio I. L. Peretz; **Izaura Valverde**, Nova Escola.

Curitiba Liana Andrade, Colégio Medianeira; **Bianca S. Borges**, Colégio Bom Jesus; **Rosana Fernandes**, Colégio Bom Jesus; **Cecilia Honorio**, Colégio Medianeira; **Regina Linzmayer**, Colégio Bom Jesus; **Maria Cecília Piccoli**, Colégio N. S. Sion; **Ana L. Z. Pinto**, Colégio Bom Jesus; **Mary C. M. dos Santos**, Colégio Bom Jesus; **Andrea S. M. Souza**, Colégio Bom Jesus; **Juçara M. S. Tadra**, Colégio Bom Jesus.

Rio de Janeiro Alcyrema R. Castro, Colégio N. S. da Assunção; **Renata Frazão**, Colégio Verbo Divino; **Claudia G. Goretti**, Colégio dos Jesuítas; **Letícia Leite**, Colégio Verbo Divino; **Livia Mercuri**, WSA Idiomas; **Marta Moraes**, Colégio São Vicente de Paulo; **Claudia C. Rosa**, Colégio Santa Mônica.

Belo Horizonte Júnia Barcelos, Colégio Santo Agostinho; **Rachel Farias**, Colégio Edna Roriz; **Renato Galil**, Colégio Santo Agostinho; **Katia R. P. A. Lima**, Colégio Santa Maria; **Gleides A. Nonato**, Colégio Arnaldo; **Luciana Queiros**, Instituto Itapoã; **Flávia Samarane**, Colégio Logosófico González Pecotche; **Adriana Zardini**, UFMG.

Brasília José Eugenio F. Alvim, CIL – 01; **Rosemberg Andrade**, Colégio Presbiteriano Mackenzie; **Euzenira Araújo**, CIL – Gama; **Michelle Câmara**, CIL – Gama; **Kátia Falcomer**, Casa Thomas Jefferson; **Almerinda B. Garibaldi**, CIL – Taguatinga; **Michelle Gheller**, CIL – Taguatinga; **Anabel Cervo Lima**, CIL – Brasília; **Ana Lúcia F. de Morais**, CIL – Brazlândia; **Antonio José O. Neto**, CIL – Ceilândia; **Maria da Graça Nóbile**, Colégio Presbiteriano Mackenzie; **Denise A. Nunes**, CIL – Gama; **Suzana Oliveira**, CIL – Taguatinga; **Andréa Pacheco**, Colégio Marista João Paulo II; **Simone Peixoto**, CIL – Brazlândia; **Érica S. Rodrigues**, Colégio Presbiteriano Mackenzie; **Isaura Rodrigues**, CIL – Ceilândia; **Camila Salmazo**, Colégio Marista João Paulo II; **Maria da Guia Santos**, CIL – Gama; **Dóris Scolmeister**, CIL – Gama; **Rejane M. C. de Souza**, Colégio Santa Rosa; **Isabel Teixeira**, CIL – Taguatinga; **Marina Vazquez**, CIL – Gama.

Questionnaires

Brazil Maria Heloísa Alves Audino, Colégio São Teodoro de Nossa Senhora de Sion; **Gleides A. Nonato**, Colégio Amaldo; **Gustavo Henrique Pires**, Instituto Presbiteriano de Educação; **Marta Gabriella Brunale dos Reis**, Colégio Integrado Jaó; **Paula Conti dos Reis Santos**, Colégio Anglo-Latino; **Tânia M. Sasaki**, High Five Language Center.

South Korea Don M. Ahn, EDLS; **Don Bryant**, OnGok Middle School.

Taiwan John A. Davey, Stella Matutina Girls' High School, Taichung City, Taiwan; **Gregory Alan Gwenossis**, Victoria Academy.

Japan Simon Butler, Fujimi Junior and Senior High School; **Yuko Hiroyama**, Pioneer Language School; **Mark Itoh**, Honjo East Senior High School Affiliated Junior High School; **Norio Kawakubo**, Yokohama YMCA ACT; **Michael Lambe**, Kyoto Girls Junior and Senior High School; **John George Lowery**, Dokkyo Junior High School/John G. Lowery School of English; **Jacques Stearn**, American Language School; **Simon Wykamp**, Hiroshima Johoku Junior and Senior High School.

Illustration Credits

Ken Batelman 66, 81, 100, 105

James Elston 6, 7, 48, 90, 98, 99, 118

Chuck Gonzales 30, 31, 42, 60, 61, 92, 93, 95, 104, 120

Kim Johnson 46, 62, 78, 79

Frank Montagna 76, 84, 85, 117

Rob Schuster 10, 48, 94, 115, 119

James Yamasaki 22, 23, 88, 89, 102, 114

Photo Acknowledgements

The authors and publishers acknowledge the following sources of copyright material and are grateful for the permissions granted. While every effort has been made, it has not always been possible to identify the sources of all the material used, or to trace all copyright holders. If any omissions are brought to our notice, we will be happy to include the appropriate acknowledgements on reprinting.

Student's Book

p. iv (Unit 1): ©Tom Grill/Corbis; p. iv (Unit 3): ©Theo Allofs/The Image Bank/Getty Images; p. iv (Unit 4): ©Jens Kuhfs/Photographer's Choice/Getty Images; p. v (Unit 6): ©Comstock/Stockbyte/Getty Images; p. v (Unit 8): ©helenecanada/iStock/Getty Images Plus/Getty Images; p. 9: ©Indeed/Getty Images; p. 12 (T): ©Alvov/Shutterstock; p. 12 (B): ©John Davis/Taxi/Getty Images; p. 13: ©Monkey Business Images/Shutterstock; p. 14 (T): ©Hemera Technologies/AbleStock.com/Getty Images Plus/Getty Images; p. 14 (B): ©Tom Grill/Corbis; p. 15: ©Guy Vanderelst/Photographer's Choice/Getty Images; p. 16 (T): ©Fabio Pili/Alamy; p. 16 (C): ©Paul Bernhardt/Alamy; p. 16 (B): ©Blue-Orange Studio/Shutterstock; p. 18 (1): ©Ildi Papp/Shutterstock; p. 18 (2): ©Frans Lemmens/Photographer's Choice/Getty Images; p. 18 (3): ©Dan Breckwoldt/Shutterstock; p. 18 (4): ©Anton_Ivanov/Shutterstock; p. 19 (T): ©Reiner Elsen/Alamy; p. 19 (B): ©Yaromir/Shutterstock; p. 20 (T): ©Dan Thornberg/Shutterstock; p. 20 (B): ©Tom Bonaventure/Photodisc/Getty Images; p. 21 (T): ©Andre M. Chang/Alamy; p. 21 (B): ©Iuoman/iStock/Getty Images Plus/Getty Images; p. 25: ©Polka Dot Images/Getty Images Plus/Getty Images; p. 26 (TR): ©Schafer &

Hill/Photolibrary/Getty Images; p. 26 (BL): ©Poelzer Wolfgang/Alamy; p. 26 (BR): ©Ian Kennedy/Shutterstock; p. 27 (T): ©Alan SCHEIN/Alamy; p. 27 (B): ©Arco Images GmbH/Alamy; p. 28: ©ANDRZEJ WOJCICKI/Science Photo Library/Getty Images; p. 29: ©Martin Child/The Image Bank/Getty Images; p. 32 (1): ©Purestock/Getty Images; p. 32 (2): ©Ammit Jack/Shutterstock; p. 32 (3): ©auremar/Shutterstock; p. 32 (4): ©Rachel Weill/Photodisc/Getty Images; p. 32 (5): ©Theo Allofs/The Image Bank/Getty Images; p. 32 (6): ©Phil Degginger/Alamy; p. 32 (7): ©Sam Chadwick/Shutterstock; p. 32 (8): ©Dmitriy Shironosov/Getty Images; p. 34: ©PhotoAlto/Alamy; p. 37 (L): ©PHAS/UIG/Getty Images; p. 37 (R): ©Everett Historical/Shutterstock; p. 38 (L): ©Corbis; p. 38 (R): ©Time Life Pictures/Mansell/The LIFE Picture Collection/Getty Images; p. 40 (T): ©Mindscape studio/Shutterstock; p. 40 (B): ©Juniors Bildarchiv GmbH/Alamy; p. 41: ©antoniodiaz/Shutterstock; p. 43 (T): ©Car Culture ® Collection/Getty Images; p. 43 (B): ©Hulton Archive/Getty Images; p. 45 (TL): ©DEA/PUBBLI AER FOTO/De Agostini Picture Library/Getty Images; p. 45 (TCL): ©Thinkstock/Stockbyte/Getty Images; p. 45 (TCR): ©javarman3/iStock/Getty Images Plus/Getty Images; p. 45 (TR): ©DP RM/Alamy; p. 45 (BL): ©Hemera Technologies/AbleStock.com/Getty Images Plus/Getty Images; p. 45 (BCL): ©uphoto/Alamy; p. 45 (BCR): ©Travel Ink/Gallo Images/Getty Images; p. 45 (BR): ©anderm/iStock/Getty Images Plus/Getty Images; p. 47 (TL): ©Alexlukin/Stock/Getty Images Plus/Getty Images; p. 47 (TCL): ©Philip Gatward/Dorling Kindersley/Getty Images; p. 47 (TCR): ©Elnur/Shutterstock; p. 47 (TR): ©Elnur/Shutterstock; p. 47 (BL): ©Nick White/Digital Vision/Getty Images; p. 47 (BCL): ©Raywoo/iStock/Getty Images Plus/Getty Images; p. 47 (BCR): ©D. Hurst/Alamy; p. 47 (BR): ©Frank Herholdt/The Image Bank/Getty Images; p. 50 (TL): ©Pal Teravagimov/Shutterstock; p. 50 (CL): ©World Perspectives/The Image Bank/Getty Images; p. 50 (BL): ©reptiles4all/Shutterstock; p. 50 (TR): ©SEBASTIAN KAULITZKI/Science Photo Library/Corbis; p. 50 (CR): ©inbj/iStock/Getty Images Plus/Getty Images; p. 50 (BR): ©44kawa/iStock/Getty Images Plus/Getty Images; p. 51 (TL): ©Rafael Ben-Ari/Alamy; p. 51 (TC): ©Maros Bauer/Shutterstock; p. 51 (TR): ©Filipe Frazao/Shutterstock; p. 51 (BL): ©DansPhotoArt on flickr/Moment Select/Getty Images; p. 51 (BC): ©Cesar Hugo Storero/Moment/Getty Images; p. 51 (BR): ©Will & Deni McIntyre/The Image Bank/Getty Images; p. 52 (TL): ©Westend61/Getty Images; p. 52 (TR): ©Iain Masterton/Alamy; p. 52 (B): ©Orhan Cam/Shutterstock; p. 54 (T): ©Dennis MacDonald/Alamy; p. 54 (B): ©STAN HONDA/AFP/Getty Images; p. 55: ©Image Source/Getty Images; p. 56 (T): ©Tom Brakefield/Digital Vision/Getty Images; p. 56 (C): ©Jens Kuhfs/Photographer's Choice/Getty Images; p. 56 (B): ©Johan Larson/iStock/Getty Images Plus/Getty Images; p. 57: ©Kevin Mazur/WireImage for Parkwood Entertainment/Getty Images; p. 59: ©Pikoso.kz/Shutterstock; p. 63: ©Bob Melnychuk/Photodisc/Getty Images; p. 64 (TL): ©Mode Images/Alamy; p. 64 (BL): ©Feng Yu/Shutterstock; p. 64 (TR): ©Caspar Benson/Getty Images; p. 64 (BR): ©studioVin/Shutterstock; p. 65 (T): ©michaeljung/Shutterstock; p. 65 (boys): ©RubberBall/Alamy; p. 65 (woman exercising): ©Jose Luis Pelaez Inc/Blend Images/Getty Images; p. 65 (B): ©Elvele Images Ltd/Alamy; p. 67 (B): ©Comstock/Stockbyte/Getty Images; p. 68: ©Knauer/Johnston/Photolibrary/Getty Images; p. 69: ©Soren Hald/The Image Bank/Getty Images; p. 70: ©Yuri_Arcurs/iStock/Getty Images Plus/Getty Images; p. 72 (TL): ©Richard G. Bingham II/Alamy; p. 72 (TC): ©Colleen Butler/iStock/Getty Images Plus/Getty Images; p. 72 (TR): ©Michael Blann/Iconica/Getty Images; p. 72 (BL): ©SW Productions/Photodisc/Getty Images; p. 72 (BC): ©Ryerson Clark/E+/Getty Images;p. 72 (BR): ©monkeybusinessimages/iStock/Getty Images Plus/Getty Images; p. 74 (1): ©Digital Vision/Photodisc/Getty Images; p. 74 (2): ©ImageGap/iStock/Getty Images Plus/Getty Images; p. 74 (3): ©marilyn barbone/Shutterstock; p. 74 (4): ©Michael Keller/Corbis; p. 74 (5): ©skynesher/Collection:iStock/Getty Images Plus/Getty Images; p. 74 (6): ©Angela Luchianiuc/Getty Images; p. 74 (7): ©Dory/Alamy; p. 74 (8): ©Anna Hoychuk/Shutterstock; p. 77 (T): ©Prapann/Shutterstock; p. 77 (B): ©Lucky Business/Shutterstock; p. 82: ©Comstock/Stockbyte/Getty Images; p. 83 (T): ©Monkey Business Images/Shutterstock; p. 83 (B): ©monkeybusinessimages/iStock/Getty Images Plus/Getty Images; p. 87 (L): ©Fuse/Getty Images; p. 87 (CL): ©Lisa-Blue/E+/Getty Images; p. 87 (CR): ©Jupiterimages/Stockbyte/Getty Images; p. 87 (R): ©Halfpoint/Shutterstock; p. 91 (L): ©MachineHeadz/iStock/Getty Images Plus/Getty Images; p. 91 (R): ©Jeff Metzger/Hemera Getty Images Plus/Getty Images; p. 96 (T): ©Aleksandra Dabrowa; p. 96 (B): ©Pefkos/Shutterstock; p. 97: ©Maria Teijeiro/Photodisc/Getty Images; p. 106 (TL): ©J. Schwanke/Alamy; p. 106 (TR): ©Richard Levine/Alamy; p. 106 (CL): ©culliganphoto/Alamy; p. 106 (CR): ©OlegAlbinsky/iStock/Getty Images Plus/Getty Images; p. 106 (BL): ©helenecanada/iStock/Getty Images Plus/Getty Images; p. 106 (BR): ©Will & Deni McIntyre/The Image Bank/Getty Images; p. 107: ©Randy Duchaine/Alamy; p. 108 (T): ©Kim Grant/Lonely Planet Images/Getty Images; p. 108 (CL): ©Ruthven Carstairs/Alamy; p. 108 (C): ©Vespasian/Alamy; p. 108 (CR): ©Clarence Holmes Photography/Alamy; p. 108 (BL): ©Darren McCollester/Newsmakers/Getty Images; p. 108 (BC): ©Universal Images Group Limited/Alamy; p. 108 (BR): ©Ferne Arfin/Alamy; p. 109: ©JL Images/Alamy; p. 110 (T): ©T photography/Shutterstock; p. 110 (B): ©Ken Welsh/Alamy; p. 111: ©Africa Studio/Shutterstock; p. 126: ©Tetra Images/Getty Images; p. 127 (T): ©Tanya Constantine/Blend Images/Getty Images; p. 127 (B): ©W Gaspar Photography/Moment/Getty Images; p. 128: ©Pictorial Press Ltd/Alamy; p. 129: ©Hung Chung Chih/Shutterstock; p. 130: ©Jack Hollingsworth/Photodisc/Getty Images; p. 131 (TL): ©Rawpixel/iStock/Getty Images Plus/Getty Images; p. 131 (CR): ©Linda Stewart/Stock/Getty Images Plus/Getty Images; p. 131 (CL): ©Gemenacom/Shutterstock; p. 131 (TR): ©Alexander Dashewsky/Shutterstock; p. 131 (BR): ©Cameramannz/Shutterstock.

Commissioned photography by Lawrence Migdale pp 2, 4, 5, 8, 11, 17, 23, 24, 33, 36, 39, 44, 58, 61, 67 (T), 75, 80, 86, 101.

Cover photograph by © A. T. Willett/Alamy

Art direction, book design, and layout services: A+ Comunicação, SP

Connect

revised edition

Jack C. Richards
Carlos Barbisan
com Chuck Sandy e
Lisa A. Hutchins

Combo 3
Workbook

CAMBRIDGE UNIVERSITY PRESS

Table of Contents

Unit 1 Back to School
- Lesson 1 New friends 2
- Lesson 2 School dinner 3
- Mini-review 4
- Lesson 3 My new school 5
- Lesson 4 After school 6
- Get Connected 7
- Check Yourself 8

Unit 2 Fun Times
- Lesson 5 Summer fun 9
- Lesson 6 Our trip to Peru 10
- Mini-review 11
- Lesson 7 School festival 12
- Lesson 8 Weekend fun 13
- Get Connected 14
- Check Yourself 15

Unit 3 Going Places
- Lesson 9 A homestay 16
- Lesson 10 Getting away 17
- Mini-review 18
- Lesson 11 Explorers 19
- Lesson 12 Up and away 20
- Get Connected 21
- Check Yourself 22

Unit 4 Comparisons
- Lesson 13 Fun facts 23
- Lesson 14 My opinion 24
- Mini-review 25
- Lesson 15 World trivia 26
- Lesson 16 The most 27
- Get Connected 28
- Check Yourself 29

Unit 5 Your Health
- Lesson 17 Yoga class 30
- Lesson 18 I don't feel well. 31
- Mini-review 32
- Lesson 19 Are you healthy? 33
- Lesson 20 Teen health tips 34
- Get Connected 35
- Check Yourself 36

Unit 6 Special Events
- Lesson 21 School fund-raiser 37
- Lesson 22 A farewell party 38
- Mini-review 39
- Lesson 23 Dance clothes 40
- Lesson 24 After the dance 41
- Get Connected 42
- Check Yourself 43

Unit 7 Our Stories
- Lesson 25 The blackout 44
- Lesson 26 Scary experiences 45
- Mini-review 46
- Lesson 27 Close calls 47
- Lesson 28 Sharing stories. 48
- Get Connected 49
- Check Yourself 50

Unit 8 In the City
- Lesson 29 How do I get there? 51
- Lesson 30 Street fair 52
- Mini-review 53
- Lesson 31 Things to do 54
- Lesson 32 We didn't go … 55
- Get Connected 56
- Check Yourself 57

Lesson 1: New friends

1 Complete the questions with *Do* or *Does* and the verbs in the box. Then answer the questions.

☐ get up   ☐ have   ☑ like   ☐ listen   ☐ play   ☐ stay up

1. **Q:** <u>Do</u> they <u>like</u> cake? **A:** (yes) <u>Yes, they do.</u>
2. **Q:** _____ you _____ tennis? **A:** (no) _____
3. **Q:** _____ he _____ early? **A:** (yes) _____
4. **Q:** _____ you _____ to salsa music? **A:** (no) _____
5. **Q:** _____ she _____ any sisters? **A:** (no) _____
6. **Q:** _____ she _____ late? **A:** (yes) _____

2 Look at the information. Then write questions and complete the answers with *Ana* or *Ben*.

Name: Ana Suarez   Age: 13

Brothers and sisters: two sisters

Things I like / don't like: I play basketball. I like ice cream. I listen to rock music. I get up at 6:30 in the morning, but I don't like to get up early.

Something interesting about me: I have a cat. His name is Gatto.

Name: Ben Harding   Age: 14

Brothers and sisters: one brother, one sister

Things I like / don't like: I like pizza. I like rap music. I play soccer. I don't like to go shopping. It's boring.

Something interesting about me: I have a new computer! I have my own Web site.

---

1. **Q:** (who) <u>Who has a cat?</u>
   A: _____ does. Her cat's name is Gatto.

2. **Q:** (how many) _____
   A: _____ has one brother.

3. **Q:** (what) _____
   A: _____ plays soccer.

4. **Q:** (how many) _____
   A: _____ has two sisters.

5. **Q:** (how) _____
   A: _____ is 14.

6. **Q:** (what) _____
   A: _____ gets up at 6:30.

7. **Q:** (what) _____
   A: _____ likes pizza.

8. **Q:** (who) _____
   A: _____ does. It's a fun Web site.

UNIT 1 Back to School

Lesson 2: School dinner

1 Complete the conversation with the sentences in the box.

- ☐ Is she making chicken and rice?
- ☐ Mom makes delicious hamburgers!
- ☐ No, she isn't.
- ☐ She's cooking dinner.
- ☑ What's she doing?
- ☐ What's she making?

Wayne Hi, Joseline. Where's Mom?
Joseline She's in the kitchen.
Wayne Hmm. _What's she doing?_
Joseline _____
Wayne Cool! _____
Joseline _____
Wayne Oh, too bad. Chicken and rice is my favorite. _____
Joseline Hamburgers and french fries.
Wayne Great! _____

2 Complete the sentences with the correct forms of the verbs in the box.

☐ eat ☐ feed ☑ have ☐ play ☐ read ☐ sleep ☐ walk ☐ watch

I'm not at school today. It's Saturday. So, I _have_ a lot of time to play. On Saturdays, I usually _____ magazines and _____ TV, but today is different. I have a new dog. His name is Max. Today, I'm going to _____ him in the park. He loves to go outside and _____ ball. Right now, I'm _____ Max some dog food. He's really cute. He _____ next to my bed at night. Oh, no! Max doesn't like his dog food, so he's _____ my mother's shoe!

Back to School 3

Lessons 1 & 2 Mini-review

1 Look at the pictures. Then write questions and answers.

1. **Q:** What sport does Paul play?
   A: *He plays basketball.*
   Q: Is he playing now?
   A: *Yes, he is.*

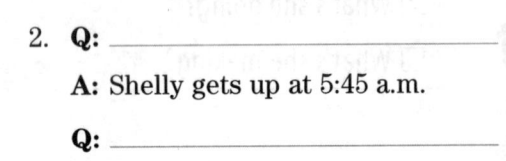

2. **Q:** _____
   A: Shelly gets up at 5:45 a.m.
   Q: _____
   A: Yes, she goes to school early.

3. **Q:** _____
   A: Bradley has three dogs.
   Q: _____
   A: No, he isn't feeding the dogs now.

4. **Q:** Who likes to skateboard?
   A: _____
   Q: Do they have skateboards?
   A: _____

2 Look at the picture of Nelly. Then write present continuous questions and short answers about her.

1. **Q:** *Is Nelly watching TV?*
   A: *No, she isn't.*

2. **Q:** _____
   A: _____

3. **Q:** _____
   A: _____

4. **Q:** _____
   A: _____

4   Unit 1

Lesson 3: My new school

1 **Write sentences with *have to* or *don't have to*. Use your own information.**

1. (wear a uniform) _I don't have to wear a uniform._
2. (clean my room) _____
3. (walk to school) _____
4. _____
5. _____

2 **Look at Leila's to-do list. She has checked the things she has to do every day. Write questions and answers about Leila's day. Use the correct forms of *have to* or *don't have to*.**

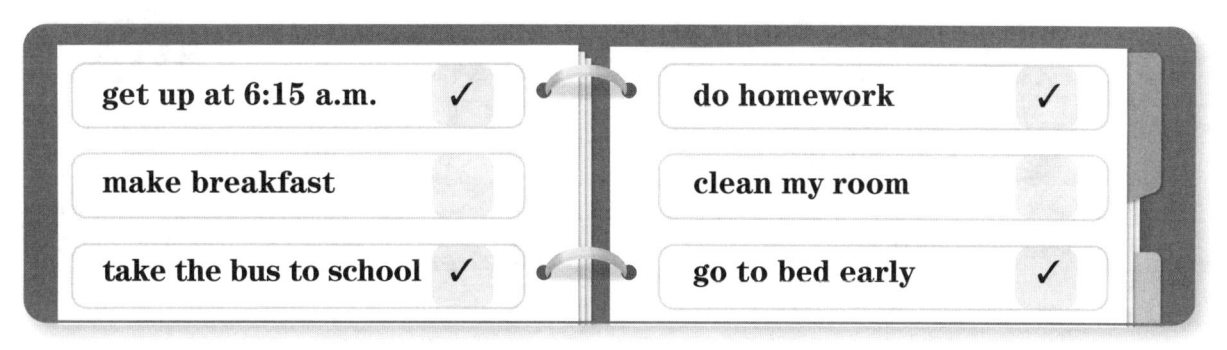

- get up at 6:15 a.m. ✓
- make breakfast
- take the bus to school ✓
- do homework ✓
- clean my room
- go to bed early ✓

1. **Q:** _Does she have to get up at 6:15 a.m.?_
   A: _Yes, she does._ OR _Yes. She has to get up at 6:15 a.m._
2. **Q:** _____
   A: _____
3. **Q:** _____
   A: _____
4. **Q:** _____
   A: _____
5. **Q:** _____
   A: _____
6. **Q:** _____
   A: _____

3 **Write questions and answers with *have to* or *don't have to*.**

1. **Q:** (students / take gym class) _Do students have to take gym class?_
   A: (yes) _Yes, they do._ OR _Yes. They have to take gym class._
2. **Q:** (teachers / buy lunch in the cafeteria) _____
   A: (no) _____
3. **Q:** (you / wear a uniform) _____
   A: (yes) _____
4. **Q:** (soccer players / practice every day) _____
   A: (no) _____

Lesson 4 — After school

1 Answer the questions with your own information.

1. Would you like to eat ice cream now? __Yes, I would.__ OR __No, I wouldn't.__
2. Would you like to make a Web site? _____
3. Would you like to make dinner tonight? _____
4. Would you like to get some exercise today? _____
5. Would you like to meet some new people? _____
6. Would you like to do your homework this afternoon? _____

2 Look at the pictures of after-school activities. Then write questions.

1. **A** _Would you like to join the volleyball club?_
   B Yes, I would.

2. **A** _____
   B Yes, I would.

3. **A** _____
   B No, I wouldn't.

4. **A** _____
   B No, I wouldn't.

5. **A** _____
   B Yes, I would.

6. **A** _____
   B Yes, I would.

6   Unit 1

UNIT 1 Get Connected

1 Read the e-mail quickly. What class is really hard?
_____

To: mrty@gc.com
From: trrnce@gc.com
Subject: College and Boston

I don't have to get up early.

Hello, Marty!
　　How are you? I'm fine, but I miss you. It's my second week here at college. I was nervous at first – I didn't know anyone. But I'm overcoming my fear and I'm starting to like it.
　　I don't have to get up early because all my classes start late. I have to do a lot of homework every day. My ecology class is really hard, but I like it.
　　Boston is an exciting city. The food is good. I'm eating crab right now at a cool little restaurant. Last weekend I learned how to row a boat and navigate it down a river. I'd like to join the boating club.
　　How is high school? Do you have to go to soccer practice every Saturday?
　　Say hi to Mom and Dad.
Your brother,
Terrance

2 Circle the correct words to complete the sentences.

1. (**crabs** / Fear) come from the ocean. I love to eat them.
2. My sister wants to study (college / ecology).
3. It's not easy to (get up / overcome my fear) of the water.
4. I'd like to (start / row) a boat down a river.

3 Read the e-mail in Part 1 slowly. Answer the questions.

1. Is Terrance overcoming his fear? _Yes, he is._
2. Does Terrance have to get up early every day? _____
3. How much homework does he have to do every day? _____
4. Does he like Boston? _____
5. What's Terrance doing right now? _____
6. Would he like to join the boating club? _____

Back to School 7

UNIT 1 Check Yourself

1 Number the sentences in the correct order.

___ No, I don't. Why?

___ Yes, I would. What movie do you want to see?

_1_ Do you have to do your homework now?

___ That sounds good to me!

___ I'd like to see *Super Dog*.

___ Would you like to go to the movies with me?

2 Write questions in the present continuous. Then answer the questions.

1. **Q:** (Shelley / play soccer) _Is Shelley playing soccer?_
   A: (no) _No, she isn't._
2. **Q:** (what / Ivan / do) _____
   A: (listen to music) _____
3. **Q:** (you / do homework) _____
   A: (yes) _____
4. **Q:** (what / Luciana / eat) _____
   A: (pizza) _____
5. **Q:** (what / Lucas / read) _____
   A: (a magazine) _____
6. **Q:** (Walter / buy comic books) _____
   A: (no) _____

3 Complete the conversations with the sentences in the box.

> ☐ Celia does.
> ☐ Does Francisco have to do homework tonight?
> ☑ He has three sisters.
> ☐ Is Mr. da Silva talking on the phone?
> ☐ No, they don't.
> ☐ She's watching her favorite TV show.
> ☐ What time does Abbie get up?
> ☐ Would you like to eat dinner now?

1. **A** How many sisters does Shawn have?
   B _He has three sisters._
2. **A** What's Stella doing?
   B _____
3. **A** _____
   B No, he doesn't.
4. **A** _____
   B Yes, I would.
5. **A** _____
   B She gets up at 6:30 a.m.
6. **A** _____
   B Yes, he is.
7. **A** Who likes pop music?
   B _____
8. **A** Do students have to eat lunch in the cafeteria?
   B _____

Lesson 5: Summer fun

1 Write the verbs in the simple past.

1. skate _____skated_____
2. ask _____
3. visit _____
4. try _____
5. rent _____
6. enjoy _____
7. listen _____
8. study _____
9. arrive _____
10. dance _____

2 Rewrite the sentences in the simple past.

1. We play basketball in the park.
   We played basketball in the park.
2. Leo cleans his room after school.
   _____
3. The students walk to school.
   _____
4. We shop at the mall on Oak Street.
   _____
5. Kathy calls her friends from the beach.
   _____
6. I stay at home on Monday night.
   _____
7. They race home after school.
   _____
8. You want to go to Venezuela.
   _____
9. She practices the piano.
   _____
10. He needs new sneakers.
    _____

3 Write sentences in the simple past about what you did last week.

1. _I played soccer at the beach._
2. _____
3. _____
4. _____
5. _____
6. _____
7. _____
8. _____

Fun Time 9

Lesson 6: Our trip to Peru

1 Match the verbs to the correct simple past forms.

1. answer __o__
2. buy ____
3. drink ____
4. eat ____
5. fly ____
6. get ____
7. give ____
8. go ____
9. have ____
10. make ____
11. meet ____
12. see ____
13. sleep ____
14. snorkel ____
15. stop ____
16. take ____
17. watch ____
18. write ____

a. gave
b. made
c. ate
d. took
e. wrote
f. had
g. snorkeled
h. drank
i. stopped
j. saw
k. bought
l. got
m. slept
n. went
o. answered
p. watched
q. flew
r. met

2 Choose the correct forms of the verbs to complete the sentences.

1. I love my new camera. I (**take**/ took) pictures all the time.
2. Carlita (meet / met) some cool people at the school dance last week.
3. Mr. Stevens travels a lot. He (flies / flew) to a different place every month.
4. They (buy / bought) a new house last summer.
5. We went to the museum. We (see / saw) a lot of beautiful paintings.
6. There's no juice in the refrigerator. I (drink / drank) it yesterday.

3 Complete the text about Laurie's trip to Mexico with the simple past.

My name's Laurie. I ___went___ (go) to Mexico with my family last summer. We _____ (fly) to Cancún and _____ (stay) in a hotel near the beach. We _____ (eat) at different restaurants every day. We _____ (try) different kinds of food. I _____ (like) the chicken mole. One day, we _____ (visit) the ruins at Chichén Itzá. The ruins are really beautiful, so I _____ (take) a lot of pictures to show my friends. My sister Tori _____ (buy) some pretty jewelry. In Cozumel, a guide _____ (give) us a tour of the island. My brother _____ (get) some cool T-shirts. We _____ (meet) a lot of nice people, and we _____ (have) a great time on our vacation.

10 Unit 2

Lessons 5 & 6 Mini-review

1 Complete the chart with the simple past forms of the verbs in the box.

☑ arrive ☐ fly ☐ listen ☐ see ☐ try
☐ dance ☐ give ☐ meet ☐ shop ☐ visit
☑ drink ☐ go ☐ plan ☐ sleep ☐ walk
☐ eat ☐ learn ☐ rent ☐ take ☐ write

Regular		Irregular	
arrived		drank	

2 Complete the sentences with the simple past forms of the verbs in the box.

☑ learn ☐ practice ☐ stay ☐ visit
☐ play ☐ race ☐ try ☐ watch

1. Jerome _____learned_____ how to surf.
2. Alicia and her sister _____ a soccer game on TV.
3. Simone _____ at a beautiful hotel.
4. Hal _____ a museum on his vacation.
5. Tomiko _____ a lot of new foods.
6. Juan and Rosario _____ English.
7. Lucy _____ volleyball on the beach.
8. Mr. Parker _____ a dune buggy down the beach.

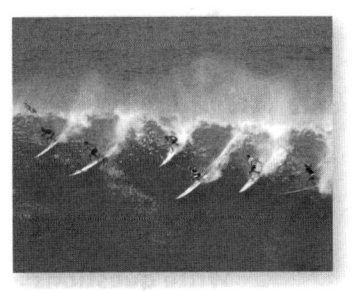

3 What did Candace do on her vacation? Write sentences.

1. (fly to Florida) _She flew to Florida._
2. (eat in many restaurants) _____
3. (go to the beach) _____
4. (buy souvenirs) _____
5. (meet new people) _____
6. (take pictures) _____
7. (write postcards) _____
8. (sleep late every day) _____

Fun Time 11

Lesson 7 — School festival

1 Look at the pictures. Then write questions and complete the answers.

1. A: *Did you win a prize?*
   B: *Yes, I did.* I won a stuffed animal.

2. A: _____
   B: _____ I went on a lot of rides.

3. A: _____
   B: _____ I don't like fun houses!

4. A: _____
   B: _____ I don't like to dance.

5. A: _____
   B: _____ I played some fun games.

6. A: _____
   B: _____ I don't like cotton candy.

2 Write questions and answers. Then match the questions to the answers.

1. exercise
   Q: *Did you exercise?* f

2. study English
   Q: _____ ___

3. buy any raffle tickets
   Q: _____ ___

4. join the chess club
   Q: _____ ___

5. win any prizes
   Q: _____ ___

6. eat cotton candy
   Q: _____ ___

a. yes / buy five raffle tickets
   A: _____

b. yes / win a stuffed animal
   A: _____

c. no / join the drama club
   A: _____

d. no / eat ice cream
   A: _____

e. no / study science
   A: _____

f. yes / run
   A: *Yes, I did. I ran.*   OR   *Yes. I ran.*

12   Unit 2

Lesson 8: Weekend fun

1 Write negative simple past sentences.

1. Danielle / go to a concert
   Danielle didn't go to a concert.

2. they / see a movie

3. Calvin / have fun on Friday

4. I / buy a new magazine

5. we / talk on the phone

6. Tony / go to a party

7. Cecilia / do a lot of homework

8. the students / go to the school festival

2 Look at Harvey's responses to a survey about weekend activities. Then write sentences about what he did and didn't do.

Check (✓) the things you did last weekend.

- ☐ play video games
- ✓ read magazines
- ☐ go to the park
- ☐ do homework
- ✓ go downtown
- ☐ talk on the phone
- ✓ listen to music
- ✓ go to a party
- ☐ eat at a restaurant
- ✓ sleep late

1. *He didn't play video games.*
2.
3.
4.
5.
6.
7.
8.
9.
10.

3 What did you do last weekend? Write four sentences about the things you did and four sentences about the things you didn't do.

1.
2.
3.
4.
5.
6.
7.
8.

Fun Time 13

UNIT 2 Get Connected

1 Read the Web site quickly. Check (✓) the animals the Web site talks about.

☐ fish   ☐ horse   ☐ parrot   ☐ tortoise
☐ frogs ☐ iguana ☐ sea lions ☐ whale

www.animalsightings.gc

Did you see any animals this summer? Tell us.

My friend and I saw a radiated tortoise at the Bronx Zoo yesterday. It wasn't a <u>giant</u> tortoise, but it was big. I also saw a lot of little red frogs. They're tomato frogs, and they're <u>endangered</u>. They're really beautiful.
– *Brian B., New York*

My family visited Mexico this summer. We went on a tour of the desert. I saw a lot of great <u>scenery</u> in the desert, but I didn't see any animals. Later at the hotel I saw an iguana in a tree in the garden. I was happy.
– *Jill C., Chicago*

In the summer I <u>went</u> to Raspberry Island in Alaska with my aunt, uncle, and cousins. We had a great time. We went on a boat tour around the island. We didn't <u>snorkel</u> – it was too cold. But we saw a lot of fish from the boat. We saw <u>sea lions</u> and a whale, too. I took pictures of the sea lions, but I didn't take any pictures of the whales. They were too far away.
– *Jim R., San Francisco*

2 Complete the conversation with the underlined words from Part 1.

Tom Where did you go this summer, Jane?
Jane I __went__ to San Diego!
Tom Did you _____ in the ocean?
Jane Yes, I did. I saw a _____ fish. It was really big!
Tom Cool! Did you see any _____ animals on your trip?
Jane No, I didn't. But I saw some _____. They're really cute.
Tom Did you enjoy the _____ there?
Jane Yes. The water and the flowers were so beautiful there.

3 Read the Web site in Part 1 slowly. Who did these things? Write *Brian*, *Jill*, or *Jim*.

1. Visited a zoo: __Brian__
2. Saw an endangered animal: _____
3. Went to an island: _____
4. Took a picture: _____
5. Traveled with family: _____ and _____
6. Went on a tour: _____ and _____

14 Unit 2

UNIT 2 Check Yourself

1 Match the questions to the answers.

1. Did Melvin go to a concert last night? __e__
2. Did you do your English homework? ____
3. Did Susanna eat lunch at 12:00? ____
4. Did Gina have a good time at the party? ____
5. Did Ann and Sid watch the fireworks? ____
6. Did Mr. Valdez buy a new camera? ____

a. Yes, she did. She had a great time at the party.
b. No. She ate lunch at 1:00.
c. No. He bought a new CD player.
d. Yes, I did. I finished my report for English.
e. No, he didn't. He went to a movie.
f. Yes. They watched them on TV.

2 Complete the sentences about Leah's vacation with the simple past.

1. (go to London) I _went to London_ .
2. (fly there) My family and I _____ .
3. (take seven hours) It _____ .
4. (visit Buckingham Palace) We _____ .
5. (buy souvenirs) My sister _____ .
6. (take great pictures) My father _____ .
7. (meet some new people) I _____ .
8. (eat good food) We _____ .

3 Steve and Flora went to a party last night. Look at the chart. Then write sentences about what they did and didn't do.

	eat pizza	dance	play games	go home early
Steve	✗	✗	✓	✗
Flora	✓	✓	✗	✓

Steve
1. _Steve didn't eat pizza._
2. _____
3. _____
4. _____

Flora
5. _____
6. _____
7. _____
8. _____

Check Yourself 15

Lesson 9: A homestay

1 Choose the correct words to complete the sentences.

1. Ellen spent the day at the beach. She was ___relaxed___ (relaxed / frustrated).
2. Kurt spilled his drink on the table. He was _____ (glad / embarrassed).
3. Ann and Al didn't pass the English test. They were _____ (frustrated / glad).
4. Ken got tickets to see his favorite rock band. He was _____ (excited / frustrated).
5. Christina didn't like flying. She was _____ (relaxed / worried).
6. We walked for eight hours. We were _____ (exhausted / embarrassed).

2 Complete Mike's e-mail message about his homestay with *was*, *were*, *wasn't*, or *weren't*.

To: **Sam**

Hi, Sam!
Well, Kevin and I made it. We flew all the way to Germany to begin our homestay. The trip was very long. Kevin ___was___ exhausted, but I _____. I _____ happy! We met our host family, Mr. and Mrs. Schmidt, at the airport. We _____ excited. They spoke English really well. We _____ surprised! I don't speak German well, but Kevin does. I _____ worried, but Kevin _____. Mr. and Mrs. Schmidt made us a great dinner. Kevin didn't like the German food. He _____ embarrassed. Mr. and Mrs. Schmidt just laughed. They _____ surprised at all. Mrs. Schmidt made Kevin some pasta. Kevin and I _____ a little homesick last night, but we're OK now. Mr. and Mrs. Schmidt are great, so we're glad to be here.
– Mike

3 Write sentences with *was* or *were*.

1. Eve / homesick
   Eve was homesick.

2. Carlo and Maria / not worried
   _____

3. Scott / glad
   _____

4. Jeremy and Max / exhausted
   _____

5. Rebecca / relaxed
   _____

6. Mr. Hill / not embarrassed
   _____

7. you / not surprised
   _____

8. Yuko / not frustrated
   _____

Lesson 10: Getting away

1 Look at the pictures. Then answer the questions.

1. **Q:** Were they at a dude ranch?
   A: *Yes, they were.*

2. **Q:** Were they at a dance club?
   A: _____

3. **Q:** Was Al at a ski resort?
   A: _____

4. **Q:** Were you on a safari?
   A: _____

5. **Q:** Was it chilly?
   A: _____

6. **Q:** Was it a big hotel?
   A: _____

2 Write questions and answers.

1. **Q:** (Sasha / at a ski resort) *Was Sasha at a ski resort?*
   A: (yes) *Yes, she was.*

2. **Q:** (Mr. and Mrs. Miller / in Brazil) _____
   A: (no) _____

3. **Q:** (the weather / nice) _____
   A: (no) _____

4. **Q:** (you / at a theme park) _____
   A: (yes) _____

5. **Q:** (your cousins / at a dude ranch) _____
   A: (no) _____

6. **Q:** (the hotel / new) _____
   A: (yes) _____

7. **Q:** (Annie / at home) _____
   A: (no) _____

Lessons 9 & 10 — Mini-review

1 Complete the sentences with was, were, wasn't, or weren't.

1. Brad fell out of the raft. He ___was___ embarrassed.
2. Adam _____ homesick. He missed his family.
3. Emilio and Juan slept a lot on Monday. They _____ exhausted on Tuesday.
4. Ted _____ nervous on the airplane. He was very relaxed.
5. Mr. and Mrs. Gray couldn't read the Japanese tour book. They _____ frustrated.
6. Sook Jin got an A on her English test. She _____ glad.

2 Complete the conversation with the sentences in the box.

☐ No, it wasn't.
☐ Was it cold?
☐ Was the weather good?
☐ Were you and your family on vacation last week?
☑ Were you on vacation last week?
☐ Yes, it was.
☐ Yes, I was.
☐ Yes, we were.

Tom Hi, Anna. _Were you on vacation last week?_
Anna _____ I was at a ski resort in Colorado.
Tom Wow! _____
Anna _____ It was very cold, and it snowed every day.
Tom That's great.
Anna How about you? _____
Tom _____ We didn't go on a trip, but we went to the Adventure Land theme park one day.
Anna _____
Tom _____ It rained. But we had a good time.

3 Write questions. Then write answers with your own information.

1. your friends / at the mall yesterday
   Q: _Were your friends at the mall yesterday?_   A: _Yes, they were._

2. the weather / nice last month
   Q: _____   A: _____

3. your English class / interesting yesterday
   Q: _____   A: _____

4. your classmates / on vacation last week
   Q: _____   A: _____

5. your best friend / in Puerto Rico last summer
   Q: _____   A: _____

Lesson 11: Explorers

1 Answer the questions.

1. **Q:** When did you travel to Colombia?
   A: (three years ago) _I traveled to Colombia three years ago._

2. **Q:** When did Sheila start her project?
   A: (two weeks ago) _____

3. **Q:** What did Ramon write about?
   A: (Spanish explorers) _____

4. **Q:** Where did you go last night?
   A: (library) _____

5. **Q:** What did they study yesterday?
   A: (math) _____

6. **Q:** Where did Mrs. Melfi go last summer?
   A: (Venezuela) _____

2 Read about Roald Amundsen. Then write questions and answers with information from the article.

> Roald Amundsen was a famous explorer. He and another explorer, Robert Scott, raced each other to the South Pole. Roald Amundsen arrived at the South Pole before Robert Scott. He arrived at the South Pole on December 14, 1911. He used 48 dogs and four sleds. Scott arrived at the South Pole a month later, in January 1912. Scott used horses on his trip to the South Pole.

1. when / Roald Amundsen / arrive at the South Pole
   Q: _When did Roald Amundsen arrive at the South Pole?_
   A: _He arrived at the South Pole on December 14, 1911._

2. what / Roald Amundsen / use on his trip
   Q: _____
   A: _____

3. when / Robert Scott / arrive at the South Pole
   Q: _____
   A: _____

4. what / Robert Scott / use on his trip
   Q: _____
   A: _____

Going Places 19

Lesson 12: Up and away

1 Look at the information. Then answer the questions about Mae Jemison.

Mae Jemison, Astronaut
- Born October 17th, 1956, in Decatur, Alabama
- Completed astronaut training in 1988
- Flew into space for the first time in 1992
- Name of shuttle was *Endeavour*
- Left NASA in 1993

1. When was Mae Jemison born? *She was born on October 17th, 1956.*
2. Where was Mae Jemison born? _____
3. What did Mae Jemison do in 1988? _____
4. When was Mae Jemison's first flight? _____
5. What was the name of the shuttle she flew on? _____
6. When did Mae Jemison leave NASA? _____

2 Complete the conversations. Use the simple past.

1. A *When was* your first trip?
   B *It was* three years ago.
   OR *My first trip was* three years ago.
2. A _____ his first train ride?
   B _____ 10 years ago.
3. A _____ you last night?
   B _____ at home.
4. A _____ they do last Saturday?
   B _____ swimming and shopping.
5. A _____ Alison go last year?
   B _____ to Mexico.
6. A _____ Alan Shepard?
   B _____ a famous astronaut.

3 Look at the underlined information. Then write questions.

1. Q: *Where were you born?* A: I was born in <u>Rio de Janeiro</u>.
2. Q: _____ A: I <u>did homework</u> and <u>went to the library</u> yesterday.
3. Q: _____ A: His English test was <u>last week</u>.
4. Q: _____ A: I visited <u>my aunt and uncle</u>.
5. Q: _____ A: <u>David and Dee</u> were at the mall.
6. Q: _____ A: My homestay was in <u>Lisbon, Portugal</u>.

UNIT 3 Get Connected

1 Read the article quickly. Underline the verbs in the simple past.

A Modern Hero

Susan Butcher is a modern hero in Alaska. She moved from Boston to Alaska in 1974. She loved dogs and dogsled racing, and she wanted to take part in the Iditarod. The Iditarod is a race with a dog team, and it's about 1,000 miles (1,610 kilometers) long.

Susan learned important skills for the race from local people. She raced a few times but didn't win until 1986. Susan also won the race in 1987, 1988, and 1990. Susan was the second woman to win the race. The first woman to win was Libby Riddles. She won the race in 1985.

In 2005, Susan got very sick, and she died in 2006. Today, the first Sunday in March in Alaska is "Susan Butcher Day."

2 Circle the word that is different.

1. journey   trip   (skill)
2. glad   happy   frustrated
3. miles   journey   kilometers
4. begins   starts   long

3 Read the article in Part 1 slowly. Answer the questions.

1. When did Susan Butcher move to Alaska? _She moved to Alaska in 1974._
2. What animal did she love? _____
3. What did Susan learn from local people? _____
4. How many times did Susan win the Iditarod? _____
5. Was she the first woman winner? _____
6. When did she die? _____

Going Places 21

UNIT 3 Check Yourself

1 Check (✓) the correct responses.

1. Were Omar and Marisol at the party?
   - ☑ No, they weren't.
   - ☐ Yes, she was.

2. When did Wally buy the book?
   - ☐ He's buying it now.
   - ☐ He bought it last week.

3. What did Elizabeth do yesterday?
   - ☐ She made a chocolate cake.
   - ☐ She's going to school.

4. Where was Janine last week?
   - ☐ She was in California.
   - ☐ She's in California.

5. Was the weather bad?
   - ☐ No, I wasn't.
   - ☐ No, it wasn't.

6. Were you homesick, Anita?
   - ☐ Yes, I was.
   - ☐ Yes, we were.

7. Where did Mia find the information?
   - ☐ She found it yesterday.
   - ☐ She found it on the Internet.

8. When was John's first day of school?
   - ☐ It was Monday.
   - ☐ Next week.

2 Complete the conversations with *was*, *wasn't*, *were*, or *weren't*.

1. Q: __Was__ it snowing yesterday?
   A: Yes, it __was__ .

2. Q: _____ they at Diana's party?
   A: Yes, they _____ .

3. Q: _____ Oliver and Sam at the mall?
   A: No, they _____ .

4. Q: _____ Martin at a dude ranch?
   A: No, he _____ .

5. Q: _____ it a fun party?
   A: Yes, it _____ !

6. Q: _____ you embarrassed?
   A: No, I _____ .

3 Look at the chart. How did Ms. Tyra's students feel about yesterday's test? Write sentences with *was*, *wasn't*, *were*, or *weren't*.

	Megan	Enzo	Shawn and Elliot
worried	✗	✓	✓
relaxed	✓	✗	✗
frustrated	✗	✓	✓

1. _Megan wasn't worried._
2. _____
3. _____
4. _____
5. _____
6. _____
7. _____
8. _____
9. _____

Lesson 13 Fun facts

1 Complete the sentences with comparative adjectives.

1. India is _hotter_ (hot) than Antarctica.
2. A dog can run _____ (fast) than a tortoise.
3. LeBron James is _____ (tall) than Tom Cruise.
4. Rio de Janiero is _____ (warm) than Anchorage, Alaska.
5. Brazil is _____ (large) than Peru.
6. An elephant is _____ (heavy) than a giraffe.
7. Iceland is _____ (cold) than Kenya.
8. The Amazon River is _____ (long) than the Ganges River in India.
9. Mount Everest is _____ (high) than Mount Kilimanjaro.
10. The moon is _____ (small) than the sun.

2 Write sentences.

1. cute: cats / rabbits
   Rabbits are cuter than cats.
2. cold: Costa Rica / Canada
   _____
3. heavy: elephants / birds
   _____
4. slow: airplanes / cars
   _____
5. big: a basketball / a baseball
   _____
6. short: a mouse / a horse
   _____
7. light: a book / a pencil
   _____
8. warm: the sun / the moon
   _____

3 Write sentences with your own information.

1. (tall) _I'm taller than my best friend._
2. (easy) _____
3. (long) _____
4. (friendly) _____
5. (big) _____
6. (busy) _____

UNIT 4 Comparisons

Lesson 14 — My opinion

1 Look at Maria's responses to the survey. Then write sentences about her opinions.

Opinion Survey

More popular	☑ rock music	☐ classical music
More entertaining	☐ movies	☑ concerts
More exciting	☑ basketball	☐ soccer
More delicious	☐ cake	☑ cookies
More difficult	☐ math	☑ English
More useful	☑ computers	☐ cell phones
More challenging	☐ surfing	☑ skateboarding
More interesting	☑ books	☐ TV

1. Rock music is more popular than classical music.
2. _____
3. _____
4. _____
5. _____
6. _____
7. _____
8. _____

2 What do you think? Write your opinions. Use comparisons with *more . . . than*.

1. entertaining: horror movies / action movies
   I think action movies are more entertaining than horror movies.

2. relaxing: a beach / a theme park
   _____

3. dangerous: white-water rafting / skiing
   _____

4. delicious: ice cream / chocolate cake
   _____

5. important: math / science
   _____

6. popular: baseball / basketball
   _____

7. useful: the Internet / books
   _____

8. challenging: speaking English / reading English
   _____

ADVENTURE MOUNTAIN

Lessons 13 & 14 — Mini-review

1 Look at the chart. Are the statements about these athletes true or false? Write T (true) or F (false). Then correct the false statements.

	LeBron James	**Rafael Nadal**	**David Wright**
Born	December 30, 1984	June 3, 1986	December 20, 1982
Height	6 feet, 8 inches (2.03 meters)	6 feet, 1 inch (1.85 meters)	6 feet, 1 inch (1.85 meters)
Weight	250 pounds (113.39 kilograms)	188 pounds (85.27 kilograms)	208 pounds (94.35 kilograms)

1. LeBron James is lighter than David Wright. __F__
   LeBron James is heavier than David Wright.

2. Rafael Nadal is shorter than LeBron James. ____
   _____

3. LeBron James is older than David Wright. ____
   _____

4. Rafael Nadal is younger than David Wright. ____
   _____

5. Rafael Nadal is heavier than LeBron James. ____
   _____

6. David Wright is taller than LeBron James. ____
   _____

2 Complete the conversation. Make sentences with the words in the box and comparative adjectives. Use *more* when necessary.

- ☐ cats / friendly / dogs
- ☐ I think dogs / friendly / cats
- ☐ I think skiing / safe / white-water rafting
- ☐ I think tennis / hard / soccer
- ☐ pasta / fast to make / pizza
- ☐ pizza / delicious / pasta
- ☑ tennis / difficult / soccer
- ☐ white-water rafting / dangerous / skiing

Rick Hi, Allison. What are you doing?

Allison I'm taking an opinion survey. Do you agree with this sentence?
Tennis is more difficult than soccer.

Rick I agree. _____

Allison OK, next item. _____

Rick I don't know. Cats are OK, but dogs are great.
_____

Allison So, you disagree. How about this one? _____

Rick White-water rafting and skiing. Hmm. _____
I guess I agree.

Allison OK. Last one. _____

Rick Wow. I like them both. But it only takes 10 minutes to make pasta.
_____
And that's important when I'm really hungry!

Lesson 15 — World trivia

1 Complete the questions with the superlative forms of the adjectives. Then answer the questions.

1. **Q:** What's _the tallest_ (tall) building in the world?
   A: (Burj Dubai) _Burj Dubai is the tallest building in the world._

2. **Q:** What's _____ (large) mall in the U.S.?
   A: (the Mall of America) _____

3. **Q:** What's _____ (hot) city in the world?
   A: (Bangkok) _____

4. **Q:** What's _____ (long) river in the world?
   A: (the Nile) _____

5. **Q:** What's _____ (heavy) snake in the world?
   A: (the anaconda) _____

2 Look at the Web site. Then write simple past questions and answers about dinosaurs. Use superlatives.

Dinosaur Trivia
- fastest dinosaur: Dromiceiomimus
- heaviest dinosaur: Argentinosaurus
- smartest dinosaur: Troodon
- tallest dinosaur: Sauroposeidon
- smallest dinosaur: Compsognathus

1. **Q:** _What was the smartest dinosaur in the world?_
   A: _The Troodon was the smartest dinosaur in the world._

2. **Q:** _____
   A: _____

3. **Q:** _____
   A: _____

4. **Q:** _____
   A: _____

5. **Q:** _____
   A: _____

Lesson 16: The most

1 Complete the article about Ms. Travel-A-Lot's opinions. Use *the most* and the adjectives in the box.

☐ beautiful ☑ exciting ☐ popular ☐ thrilling
☐ crowded   ☐ expensive ☐ relaxing

I love to travel. I travel all over the world. Here are some of my favorite places. I think Bangkok is _the most exciting_ city in the world. It has fantastic stores, restaurants, and museums. There's always something to do in Bangkok. _____ city in the world is San Francisco. The Golden Gate Bridge and its many parks and gardens make San Francisco a pretty city to visit. I think New York City is _____ city in the United States. In some places, a slice of pizza is five dollars! _____ city in the world is Honolulu. You can sit on Waikiki Beach and enjoy the sun and sand. _____ city in the world is Las Vegas. There are great theme parks to visit, and some hotels even have their own roller coasters! _____ city in the world is Mumbai, India. There are almost 14 million people in Mumbai! And finally, Paris is _____ city in the world. More tourists visit Paris each year than any other city in the world!

2 Write questions and answers.

1. popular city in Brazil / Rio de Janeiro
   Q: _What's the most popular city in Brazil?_
   A: _Rio de Janeiro is the most popular city in Brazil._
   OR _The most popular city in Brazil is Rio de Janeiro._

2. beautiful city in Canada / Vancouver
   Q: _____
   A: _____

3. famous statue in New York City / the Statue of Liberty
   Q: _____
   A: _____

4. exciting city in Japan / Kyoto
   Q: _____
   A: _____

5. expensive city in the world / Moscow
   Q: _____
   A: _____

UNIT 4   Get Connected

1 Read the Web site quickly. Match the pictures to the facts in the Web site.

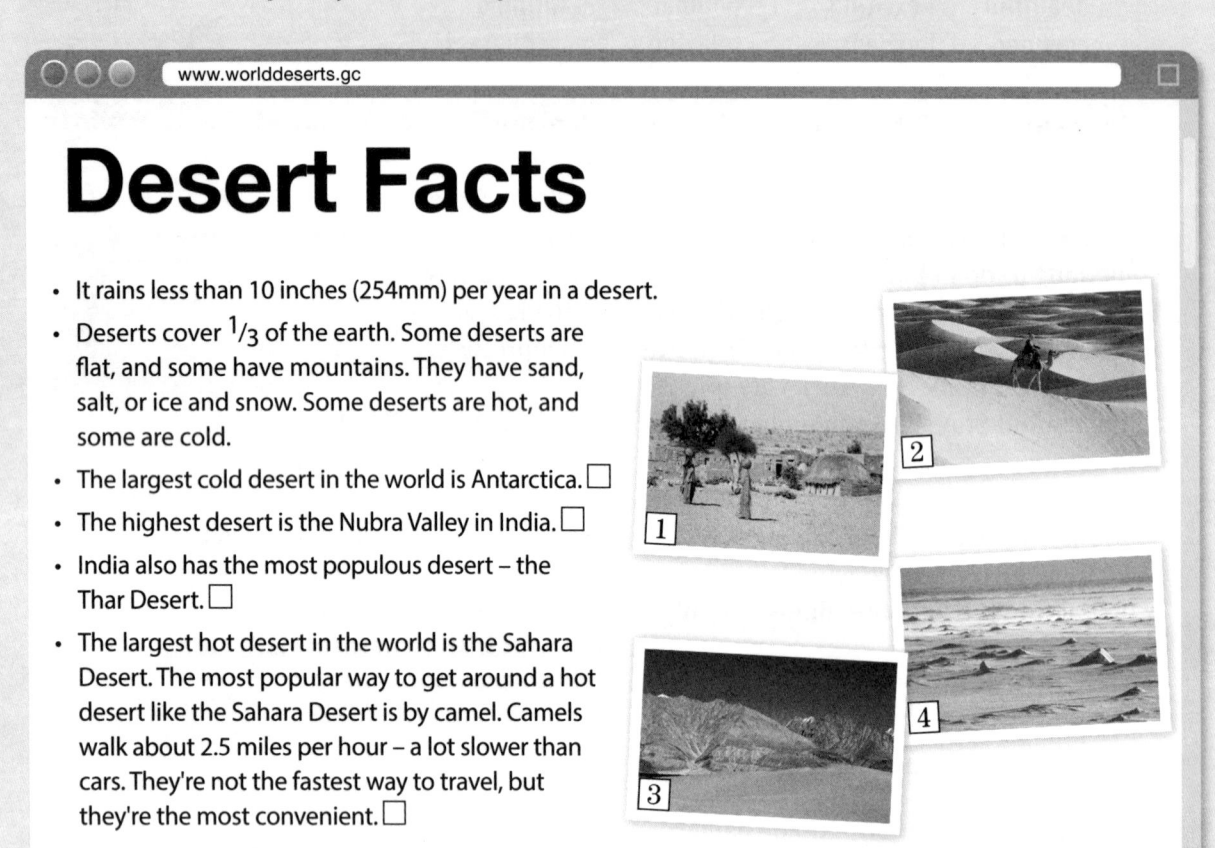

www.worlddeserts.gc

Desert Facts

- It rains less than 10 inches (254mm) per year in a desert.
- Deserts cover ⅓ of the earth. Some deserts are flat, and some have mountains. They have sand, salt, or ice and snow. Some deserts are hot, and some are cold.
- The largest cold desert in the world is Antarctica. ☐
- The highest desert is the Nubra Valley in India. ☐
- India also has the most populous desert – the Thar Desert. ☐
- The largest hot desert in the world is the Sahara Desert. The most popular way to get around a hot desert like the Sahara Desert is by camel. Camels walk about 2.5 miles per hour – a lot slower than cars. They're not the fastest way to travel, but they're the most convenient. ☐

2 Circle the correct words to complete the sentences.

1. My mother likes to climb (**mountains** / deserts).
2. The (heaviest / tallest) building in New York City is the Freedom Tower.
3. My sister is the (fastest / highest) driver in the family.
4. The most (popular / populous) snack in the world is potato chips.

3 Read the Web site in Part 1 slowly. Correct the underlined words in the sentences.

1. Deserts cover ½ of the earth.   [⅓]
2. Antarctica is <u>hotter</u> than the Sahara.
3. <u>The Thar Desert</u> is higher than all other deserts.
4. <u>The Nubra Valley</u> is the most populous desert in the world.
5. Camels are the most <u>dangerous</u> way to get around in a desert.
6. Camels are <u>faster</u> than cars.

28 Unit 4

UNIT 4 Check Yourself

1 **Number the sentences in the correct order.**

_____ Really? Why do you think he's the most famous actor in the world?

_____ Yes, they are. Now, Sabrina, who's the most beautiful actress in the world?

_____ OK. I agree with you. They're also some of the most thrilling movies around.

_____ Well, I think Tobey Maguire is the most famous actor in the world.

_____ Hmm. I think Penelope Cruz is the most beautiful actress in the world.

_____ He starred in the *Spider-Man* movies. They're some of the most popular movies around.

__1__ Sondra, who's the most famous actor in the world?

2 **Complete the texts with comparative adjectives. Use *more* when necessary.**

1. Hi. I'm Monica. I'm 14. I have a sister. Her name is Melissa. She's ___younger___ (young) than I am, but she's _____ (tall) than I am. My favorite subject is science. I think it's _____ (easy) than English. I like pop music, but my sister likes rap. She thinks rap music is _____ (popular) than pop. My sister likes movies, but I don't. I think concerts are _____ (entertaining) than movies.

2. Hello! I'm Jaime. I just moved to Houston from New York City. Houston is _____ (warm) than New York City, but I think New York City is _____ (busy) than Houston. My favorite sport is soccer. It's _____ (exciting) than baseball! Soccer players run _____ (fast) than baseball players. Soccer is _____ (hard) to play, too!

3 **Write questions and answers about these students in Mrs. Turner's class. Use superlatives.**

| Hank | Lorena | Brian | Jin |

1. **Q:** (fast girl) _Who's the fastest girl in Mrs. Turner's class?_
   A: _Jin is the fastest girl in Mrs. Turner's class._
2. **Q:** (strong boy) _____
   A: _____
3. **Q:** (smart girl) _____
   A: _____
4. **Q:** (tall boy) _____
   A: _____

Check Yourself 29

Lesson 17: Yoga class

1 Write the adverbs of manner for the adjectives.

1. comfortable ___comfortably___
2. regular _____
3. careful _____
4. quick _____
5. slow _____
6. crazy _____
7. quiet _____
8. happy _____
9. important _____
10. easy _____

2 Complete the sentences with the correct forms of the adjectives in the box.

☑ careful ☐ comfortable ☐ patient ☐ quick ☐ quiet ☐ regular

1. I helped my mom make a cake. She told me to measure the flour ___carefully___.
2. Our gym teacher told us to dress _____ today. We're learning yoga.
3. Please don't make noise in the library. Study _____.
4. I go to the gym _____. I go every day.
5. Dr. Cole will see you in a few minutes. Please wait _____.
6. Warren can read one book a day. He reads _____.

3 Look at the pictures. Then write sentences with adverbs of manner.

☐ careful / crazy ☐ loud / quiet ☑ quick / slow ☐ safe / dangerous

1. (run) ___Judy runs quickly. Min runs slowly.___
2. (sing) _____
3. (ride his bike) _____  
4. (dance) _____

Lesson 18: I don't feel well.

1 Choose the correct words to complete the sentences.

1. Where are my eyedrops? My ___allergies___ (sore throat / allergies) are terrible today.
2. I have _____ (a cold / a headache). My head really hurts.
3. I talked too much today. I have _____ (a sore throat / the flu).
4. When I have _____ (the flu / a headache), I eat some chicken soup.
5. I have _____ (allergies / an earache), so my doctor gave me some eardrops.
6. I drink a lot of water when I have _____ (an earache / a cold).

2 Write questions and answers.

1. **Q:** (you / have an earache) _What do you do when you have an earache?_
   A: (use warm eardrops) _I use warm eardrops when I have an earache._
   OR _When I have an earache, I use warm eardrops._

2. **Q:** (Julio / have a sore throat) _____
   A: (drink hot tea with lemon) _____

3. **Q:** (Linda / have a headache) _____
   A: (try to rest in a quiet place) _____

4. **Q:** (Mr. and Mrs. Wells / have colds) _____
   A: (drink a lot of water) _____

5. **Q:** (you / have allergies) _____
   A: (take some allergy pills) _____

3 Complete the conversation.

Wendell I don't feel well. I have a cold, a sore throat, and an earache.
Mom Oh, no! That's too bad!
Wendell (have a cold) _What do you do when you have a cold?_
Mom (take some cold medicine) _____
Wendell OK. (a sore throat) _____
Mom (drink hot tea with lemon) _____
Wendell Yuck! That sounds terrible. (an earache) _____
_____
Mom (go to the doctor) _____
Wendell The doctor? Oh, no! I don't like to go to the doctor.
Mom I know. But you need some eardrops, so I'm calling the doctor right now!

Lessons 17 & 18 Mini-review

1 Complete the weight-training tips with adverbs of manner.

Health & Fitness

Weight training is very important. When you lift weights, you make your muscles stronger. Strong muscles can help you run faster and jump higher when you play sports. Read these tips:

- You can ___easily___ (easy) begin a weight-training program in a gym or a health club.
- Most gyms and health clubs have trainers who can show you how to do each exercise _____ (safe) and _____ (correct).
- Dress _____ (comfortable). Wear sneakers and loose clothing.
- Begin your weight-training program _____ (slow). Start with a few simple exercises.
- Take your time doing each exercise. Don't do the exercises _____ (quick), or you can hurt yourself.
- Go to the gym _____ (regular). It's important to train two to three times a week for the best results.
- Have fun! You're on your way to a strong, healthy body.

2 Look at the chart. Then write questions and answers.

	A cold	Allergies
Melissa	take cold medicine	take allergy pills
Manuel and Derek	drink a lot of water	stay inside
Natsuko	drink orange juice	use eyedrops

1. **Q:** _What does Melissa do when she has a cold?_
   A: _She takes cold medicine when she has a cold._
   OR _When she has a cold, she takes cold medicine._

2. **Q:** _____
   A: _____

3. **Q:** _____
   A: _____

4. **Q:** _____
   A: _____

5. **Q:** _____
   A: _____

6. **Q:** _____
   A: _____

Lesson 19 — Are you healthy?

1 Complete the sentences with the words in the box.

☐ every day   ☐ once a week   ☐ three times a week   ☐ twice a year
☐ every month   ☐ once a year   ☑ twice a day   ☐ never

1. William brushes his teeth __twice a day__. He brushes them in the morning. Then he brushes them again before he goes to bed.
2. I go to the doctor for a checkup _____. I usually go once in January and once in July.
3. Kyle feeds his dog, Rex, _____. He usually feeds Rex in the morning.
4. I celebrate my birthday _____, on August 29.
5. Liz goes to her violin lesson _____. It's at 4:00 p.m. every Wednesday.
6. Sara has soccer practice _____ – every Monday, Tuesday, and Thursday.
7. I don't like vegetables at all! I _____ eat them.
8. My parents pay their bills _____ – usually at the end of the month.

2 Look at Miguel's responses to a survey about health. Then write sentences.

Green Street Fitness

How often do you … ?			
exercise	☐ every day	☒ three times a week	☐ once a week
go to the doctor for a checkup	☒ once a year	☐ twice a year	☐ never
get a cold or the flu	☐ once a year	☒ three times a year	☐ five or more times a year
brush your teeth	☐ once a day	☒ twice a day	☐ three times a day
eat fruits and vegetables	☐ every day	☐ four or more times a week	☒ never
eat candy and cookies	☒ every day	☐ four or more times a week	☐ never

1. _He exercises three times a week._
2. _____
3. _____
4. _____
5. _____
6. _____

3 Write questions. Then answer the questions with your own information.

1. **Q:** (have a cold) _How often do you have a cold?_   **A:** _I have a cold about three times a year._
2. **Q:** (do yoga) _____   **A:** _____
3. **Q:** (brush your teeth) _____   **A:** _____
4. **Q:** (eat junk food) _____   **A:** _____
5. **Q:** (see the school nurse) _____   **A:** _____
6. **Q:** (go to the dentist) _____   **A:** _____

Lesson 20 — Teen health tips

1 Complete the sentences with *should* or *shouldn't*.

1. It's important to eat a healthy breakfast every morning. You _shouldn't_ skip breakfast.
2. You _____ protect your skin. Use sunscreen every day, even in the winter!
3. You _____ sit around and watch TV all day. Be active. Try to exercise for 30 minutes every day.
4. You _____ brush and floss your teeth regularly. It prevents cavities.
5. Eat snacks like fruit, cheese, and vegetables. You _____ eat junk food.
6. You _____ challenge your brain. Read an interesting book or do a crossword puzzle.

2 Complete the conversations. Write sentences with *should* or *shouldn't* and the verb phrases in the box.

☑ eat junk food
☐ stay up late
☐ join the drama club
☐ take an aspirin
☐ read this new book
☐ try some chicken soup
☐ skip breakfast
☐ try yoga

1. A I'm hungry. I want some cookies.
   B _You shouldn't eat junk food._ Have an apple.
2. A I feel terrible. I have the flu.
   B _____
3. A I have a headache.
   B _____
4. A I'm always tired.
   B _____
5. A I eat breakfast about three times a week.
   B Eat breakfast every day. _____
6. A I need to relax.
   B _____ It's very relaxing.
7. A I want to join a club at school.
   B _____ It's a lot of fun.
8. A I'm bored. I don't know what to do.
   B _____ It's really good!

3 What should you do to be healthy? What shouldn't you do? Write sentences.

1. _You shouldn't eat junk food._
2. _____
3. _____
4. _____
5. _____
6. _____

UNIT 5 Get Connected

1 Read the blog quickly. Write the best title in the blog.

1. A new Capoeira fan
2. Studying a martial art is hard.
3. Karate is exciting.

www.capoeirablog.gc/

Title: _____

Posted by: Petra

I wanted to move more flexibly and think more clearly, so I took a few martial arts classes. I went regularly and practiced patiently, but I didn't really like them – they weren't fun. Then a friend said, "You should try Capoeira." I did, and I love it. Capoeira is a martial art for <u>self-defense</u>, and includes music, singing, and dancing.

I go to class four times a month, and <u>practice</u> once a week at home. At first, it was difficult, but I followed my teacher's instructions carefully, and now I can do the moves more comfortably.

In class when we learn something new, we move slowly. But when we practice moves, we usually move fast, so we sometimes forget what to do! My teacher says we shouldn't worry about that. She says that we should just enjoy every class. And we do.

I can see some of the <u>benefits</u> of studying Capoeira. It's good for <u>self-esteem</u> and <u>discipline</u>, and it's a lot of fun. When you have the chance, you should try it!

2 Complete the sentences with the underlined words from Part 1.

1. When you do martial arts regularly, you will see the ___benefits___ quickly. You will feel healthier, and your _____ will probably improve, too.
2. You need to _____ a lot to become really good at a martial art.
3. Capoeira is a kind of martial art and teaches _____ skills.
4. To practice something every day you need _____ .

3 Read the blog in Part 1 slowly. Circle the correct words to complete the sentences.

1. Petra didn't like (**her martial arts classes** / her patient practice / her teacher).
2. A friend told her about (philosophy / Capoeira / self-defense).
3. She practices (four times a week / four times a month / once a week).
4. When they practice moves, they move (quickly / comfortably / slowly).
5. Petra's teacher thinks it's important to (join / study / enjoy every class).

Your Health 35

UNIT 5 Check Yourself

1 Complete the conversation with *should* or *shouldn't*.

Nicole Hi, Jason. How was your checkup? What did the doctor tell you?

Jason My checkup was OK. She gave me a lot of information.

Nicole Like what?

Jason Well, I exercise twice a week, but I _should_ exercise at least five times a week. Also, I _____ skip breakfast. I _____ eat a big, healthy breakfast every day.

Nicole How about sleep?

Jason I _____ stay up late. I _____ sleep at least eight hours every night.

Nicole What did the doctor say about candy and soda?

Jason The doctor said I _____ eat too much candy. She also said that I _____ drink water or milk instead of soda.

Nicole That makes sense.

Jason And she said I _____ relax a little every day.

2 Rewrite the sentences with adverbs of manner.

1. My sister and her friend are quick runners. _They run quickly._
2. Roberta is a slow reader. _____
3. Mrs. Patterson is a careful driver. _____
4. We need to dress in comfortable clothes. _____
5. Raquel is a loud singer. _____
6. Mr. Viera is a patient teacher. _____
7. My friend is a quiet speaker. _____
8. Joanna and Rob are regular exercisers. _____

3 Complete the conversations with the sentences in the box.

- ☐ He studies every day.
- ☐ She takes two aspirin.
- ☐ How often does Hugh exercise?
- ☑ What do you do when you're hungry?
- ☐ I never eat candy.
- ☐ What do your friends do when they have the flu?

1. **A** _What do you do when you're hungry?_
   B I ask my mother to make me a sandwich.

2. **A** What does Kendra do when she has a headache?
   B _____

3. **A** _____
   B He exercises a lot! He runs every day.

4. **A** How often do you eat candy?
   B _____

5. **A** _____
   B They stay in bed and sleep when they have the flu.

6. **A** How often does he study?
   B _____

Lesson 21

School fund-raiser

1 Look at the Roberts family's to-do list. Then write sentences with *be going to*.

Saturday To-Do List
do yard work – Mom and Frank
wash windows – Vicky
clean the garage – Dad and Brad
wash the car – Brad
walk dogs – Lisa
do homework – Frank and Brad
make dinner – Mom
babysit – Vicky

1. *Mom and Frank are going to do yard work.*
2. _____
3. _____
4. _____
5. _____
6. _____
7. _____
8. _____

2 Look at the pictures. Then write questions and answers about what these teens are going to do.

1. Lucinda / work at the bake sale
   Q: *Is Lucinda going to work at the bake sale?*
   A: *Yes, she is.*

2. Ken / do yard work
   Q: _____
   A: _____

3. Hitomi / make dinner
   Q: _____
   A: _____

4. Chris and Brian / clean the garage
   Q: _____
   A: _____

5. Matt / wash windows
   Q: _____
   A: _____

6. Lin and Nancy / walk dogs
   Q: _____
   A: _____

UNIT 6 Special Events

Special Events 37

Lesson 22 — A farewell party

1 Look at the underlined information. Then write questions to complete the conversations.

1. A *Who's going to serve the pizza?*
   B Paulo is going to serve the pizza.

2. A _____
   B We're going to have the party in the library.

3. A _____
   B Everyone is going to sign the card.

4. A _____
   B We're going to eat sandwiches.

5. A _____
   B Belle is going to wrap the gift.

6. A _____
   B Alexa is going to pour the drinks.

7. A _____
   B We're going to have the party at 12:00 p.m.

8. A _____
   B We're going to set up the snack table over there.

2 Write questions and answers to complete the conversation.

Pamela Hi, Cruz. Let's talk about the farewell party for Mr. Brady.

Cruz Great. (when / we / have the party) *When are we going to have the party?*

Pamela (next Friday) *We're going to have the party next Friday.*   OR *Next Friday.*

Cruz OK. (what / we / eat) _____

Pamela (pizza and chocolate cake) _____

Cruz Mmm. I love chocolate cake.

Pamela (where / we / have the party) _____

Cruz (the cafeteria) _____

Pamela (who / decorate the cafeteria) _____

Cruz (Cindy and Mark) _____

Pamela Good. (I / give a speech) _____

Cruz OK. (who / make the cake) _____

Pamela (you) _____

Cruz Me? I can't make cakes!

38 Unit 6

Lessons 21 & 22 — Mini-review

1 Read the article. Then write questions and answers.

Famous movie stars Mitch Ford and Jessica (Jes) Palmer have exciting plans for the weekend. They're going to go to a fancy party in Los Angeles. Jes and Mitch are going to fly to Los Angeles on Friday night. On Saturday morning, Jes is going to go shopping for a dress to wear to the party. Mitch is going to hang out with his friends. On Saturday afternoon, Jes and Mitch are going to talk to some TV reporters. On Saturday night, Jes and Mitch are going to go to the party. Jes is going to eat some fancy food, but Mitch isn't. He doesn't like fancy food. After the party, Jes and Mitch are going to fly home.

1. Jes and Mitch / go to a party
   Q: _Are Jes and Mitch going to go to a party?_
   A: _Yes, they are._

2. Jes / go shopping
   Q: _____
   A: _____

3. Mitch / hang out with his brother
   Q: _____
   A: _____

4. Jes and Mitch / go to the movies
   Q: _____
   A: _____

5. Mitch / eat some fancy food
   Q: _____
   A: _____

6. Jes and Mitch / fly home after the party
   Q: _____
   A: _____

2 What are these teens' plans for tomorrow? Look at the chart. Write *Who, What,* or *Where* questions with *be going to*. Then answer the questions.

Who	What	Where
Selina	go shopping	at the mall
Anthony	walk dogs	in the park
Owen	do homework	at the library

1. **Q:** _What's Selina going to do?_
   A: _Selina is going to go shopping._

2. **Q:** _____
   A: _____

3. **Q:** _____
   A: _____

4. **Q:** _____
   A: _____

5. **Q:** _____
   A: _____

6. **Q:** _____
   A: _____

Lesson 23: Dance clothes

1 Look at the pictures. Then complete the conversations with *Which one, Which ones, the one,* or *the ones* and the words in the box.

☐ denim ☐ flowered ☐ plaid ☐ polka-dot ☑ striped ☐ tie-dyed

1. **A** _Which one_ is Olivia?
   B She's _the one_ in the _striped_ dress.

2. **A** _____ are Mr. and Mrs. Parker?
   B They're _____ in the _____ jackets.

3. **A** _____ is Armando?
   B He's _____ in the _____ tie.

4. **A** _____ are the Ramirez brothers?
   B They're _____ in the _____ shirts.

5. **A** _____ is Lynn?
   B She's _____ in the _____ hat.

6. **A** _____ is Randy?
   B He's _____ in the _____ T-shirt.

2 Write questions and answers.

1. **Q:** (Angelo) _Which one is Angelo?_
   A: (polka-dot socks) _He's the one in the polka-dot socks._

2. **Q:** (José) _____
   A: (solid jacket) _____

3. **Q:** (Lois and Isabelle) _____
   A: (plaid skirts) _____

4. **Q:** (Rosalie) _____
   A: (flowered pants) _____

5. **Q:** (Mr. and Mrs. Clayson) _____
   A: (checked shirts) _____

Lesson 24: After the dance

1 Look at the picture. Then write questions. Match the questions to the answers.

1. denim jacket
   Q: _Whose denim jacket is this?_ _f_
2. sneakers
   Q: _____
3. hat
   Q: _____
4. comic books
   Q: _____
5. skateboard
   Q: _____
6. books
   Q: _____

a. They're Juan's.
b. It's Mel's.
c. They're Candy's.
d. It's Delilah's.
e. They're Leo's.
f. It's Viv's.

2 Look at the pictures. Then write questions and answers. Use possessive pronouns.

1. **Q:** (camera) _Whose camera is this?_
   A: _It's ours._

2. **Q:** (sunglasses) _____
   A: _____

3. **Q:** (cell phone) _____
   A: _____

4. **Q:** (cat) _____
   A: _____

5. **Q:** (backpack) _____
   A: _____

6. **Q:** (wallet) _____
   A: _____

Special Events

UNIT 6 Get Connected

1 Read the messages on the Web site quickly. What's Juanita's local library going to do?

_____

www.earthdaythisyear.gc

What are you going to do for Earth Day? Tell us about it.

NancyPlanet
My neighborhood is going to have an Earth Walk. The newspapers are telling people to walk everywhere they can on Earth Day. My parents are going to walk to work. I'm going to walk to school. My brother can't walk to his job – it's too far – but he's going to ride his bike. Stores are going to donate water and snacks for people.

Matt14C
We're going to have a fund-raiser at our school. We're going to sell organic snacks. We're going to sell tie-dyed T-shirts, too. They say, "Save the Earth!" We're also going to sell denim hats that say, "Green is Good." We'll use the money to buy big recycling bins for our school.

JuanitaVerde
The local library is going to have an art contest for Earth Day. Anyone 12 to 102 can enter! You have to make art with used things only. My best friend and I are going to make a tree with used computer ink cartridges and my father's old ties. Ten winners will have their art in the library all year!

2 Match the words to the definitions.

1. cartridge __d__
2. used _____
3. fund-raiser _____
4. organic _____
5. donate _____

a. give for free
b. natural
c. an event to get money
d. a case that holds something
e. not new

3 Read the messages in Part 1 slowly. Answer the questions.

1. Who's going to walk to school? _Nancy is going to walk to school._ OR _Nancy is._ OR _Nancy._
2. How's Nancy's brother going to get to work? _____
3. Whose school is going to sell clothing? _____
4. Who's going to enter the art contest? _____
5. What's the tree going to be made with? _____

UNIT 6 Check Yourself

1 Look at the party invitation. Then write questions and answers. Look at the underlined information for help.

Party!

To all students:
Please come to a farewell party for Mr. Connor.

When: Friday, November 7

Where: The school library

Pizza, soda, and chocolate cake for everyone! Please sign Mr. Connor's card before the party.

Stay for Mrs. Barber's speech and a special dance by the Spanish club. The teachers are going to give Mr. Connor a farewell gift.

Everyone: Please stay after the party to help clean up.

1. **Q:** Where are the students going to have the party?
   A: _They're going to have the party in the school library._ OR _In the school library._
2. **Q:** _____
   A: Mrs. Barber is going to <u>give a speech</u>.
3. **Q:** _____
   A: The Spanish club is going to <u>perform a special dance</u>.
4. **Q:** _____
   A: <u>The teachers</u> are going to give Mr. Connor a farewell gift.
5. **Q:** _____
   A: <u>Everyone</u> is going to stay after the party to help clean up.
6. **Q:** What are the students going to eat?
   A: _____
7. **Q:** Are the students going to drink tea?
   A: _____
8. **Q:** What are the students going to do before the party?
   A: _____

2 Look at the picture. Then complete the conversations. For numbers 3–5, use the correct possessive pronouns.

Rick | Paola | Ty | Aiko and Aki | Me

1. **A** (sunglasses) _Whose sunglasses are these?_
   B They're Rick's.
   A Which one is Rick?
   B _He's the one in the checked shirt._

2. **A** (necklace) _____
   B It's Paola's.
   A Which one is Paola?
   B _____

3. **A** (sneakers) _____
   B They're ___his___.
   A Which one is he?
   B _____

4. **A** (hats) _____
   B They're _____.

5. **A** (jacket) _____
   B It's _____.

Check Yourself 43

Lesson 25: The blackout

1 Complete the sentences with the affirmative or negative past continuous forms of the verbs in the box.

☐ babysit ☐ (not) do ☑ listen to ☐ make dinner ☐ play ☐ (not) read ☐ talk ☐ watch

1. Cecilia _was listening to_ an MP3 player in her room.
2. Drew _____ his homework.
   He _____ video games.
3. They _____ an exciting tennis match.
4. Sheila _____ a book.
   She _____ on her cell phone.
5. He _____ his little brother.
6. Mrs. Walker _____ in the kitchen.

2 What were the people in the pictures doing yesterday? Write past continuous sentences. Use the negative forms of the verbs when necessary.

1. (Tim and Jim / watch TV at home) _Tim and Jim weren't watching TV at home. They were riding a roller coaster._
2. (Rita / shop at the mall) _____ 
3. (Manik / do yard work) _____ 
4. (Jin and Lynn / walk dogs) _____ 
5. (you / ride your bike in the park) _____ 
6. (Kendra / take pictures with her new camera) _____

Lesson 26 — Scary experiences

1 Choose the correct forms of the verbs to complete the sentences.

1. Tara ___fell___ (was falling / fell) when she ___was skateboarding___ (was skateboarding / skateboarded).
2. We _____ (ate / were eating) lunch when the fire alarm _____ (was ringing / rang).
3. I _____ (was listening / listened) to music when I _____ (fell / was falling) asleep!
4. They _____ (watched / were watching) TV when a man _____ (was knocking / knocked) on the door.
5. Mrs. Montoya _____ (was making / made) lunch when the baby _____ (started / was starting) to cry.
6. The man _____ (was shouting / shouted) when we _____ (arrived / were arriving) at the zoo.

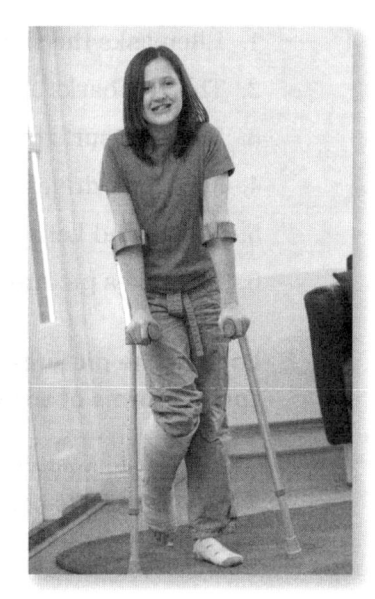

2 Look at the chart. Then write sentences with *when*. Use the correct forms of the verbs or verb phrases in the chart.

Name	Action in progress	Action completed
1. Carlos and Trina	drive to work	see a cat in the street
2. Beth	sleep	someone knock at the door
3. Diego	watch TV	the phone ring
4. Anna and Mariano	make dinner	the electricity go out
5. Tom	play soccer	fall and hurt his leg

1. ___Carlos and Trina were driving to work when they saw a cat in the street.___
2. _____
3. _____
4. _____
5. _____

3 Complete the statements with the simple past or the past continuous. Use your own information.

1. I was _____ when the alarm clock rang this morning.
2. When I got home yesterday, _____.
3. When I arrived at school this morning, _____.
4. I was _____ when the phone rang yesterday.

Our Stories 45

Lessons 25 & 26 Mini-review

1 Rewrite the sentences in the past continuous.

1. Ellen asks the singer for an autograph. _Ellen was asking the singer for an autograph._
2. The dog barks at the bird in the tree. _____
3. Eduardo surfs the Internet for information. _____
4. Mr. Lauer drives his kids to soccer practice. _____
5. Nicole and Lena talk on the phone. _____
6. Roy takes pictures of his family. _____

2 Look at the pictures. Then complete the sentences with *when* and the correct forms of the verb phrases in the box.

- ☐ do his homework / hear a noise
- ☑ in-line skate / start to rain
- ☐ wind start to blow / do yard work
- ☐ electricity go out / play a video game
- ☐ eat dinner / phone ring
- ☐ watch TV / fall asleep

1. Wendy _was in-line skating when it started to rain_ .
2. Beto _____ . 
3. Mr. and Mrs. Thomas _____ . 
4. Abi _____ . 
5. _____, we _____ . 
6. _____, Doug _____ . 

46 Unit 7

Close calls

Write questions to complete the conversations.

1. (they / skateboard) Q: _Were they skateboarding?_ A: Yes, they were.
2. (you / walk) Q: _____ A: We were walking in the park.
3. (it / rain) Q: _____ A: Yes, it was.
4. (you / do) Q: _____ A: We were white-water rafting.
5. (they / surf) Q: _____ A: No, they weren't.
6. (you / play) Q: _____ A: We were playing basketball.
7. (Sheila / study) Q: _____ A: She was studying in the library.
8. (the sun / shine) Q: _____ A: No, it wasn't.

Read the story. Then complete the questions with the past continuous. Answer the questions.

A year ago, Marty Long and his one-year-old cousin were playing together in the backyard. Marty's small dog, Zoey, was with them. It was a nice, hot summer day and they were all having a good time.

While they were playing, Zoey suddenly started running toward Marty's cousin and barking loudly. Marty ran to them and saw Zoey between the little boy and a big rattlesnake! Zoey was trying to stop the rattlesnake from biting Marty's cousin. Sadly, the snake bit Zoey on the head. Marty quickly took her to a nearby animal hospital, and a few days later she was fine. Zoey's story is now on a Web site for pet heroes.

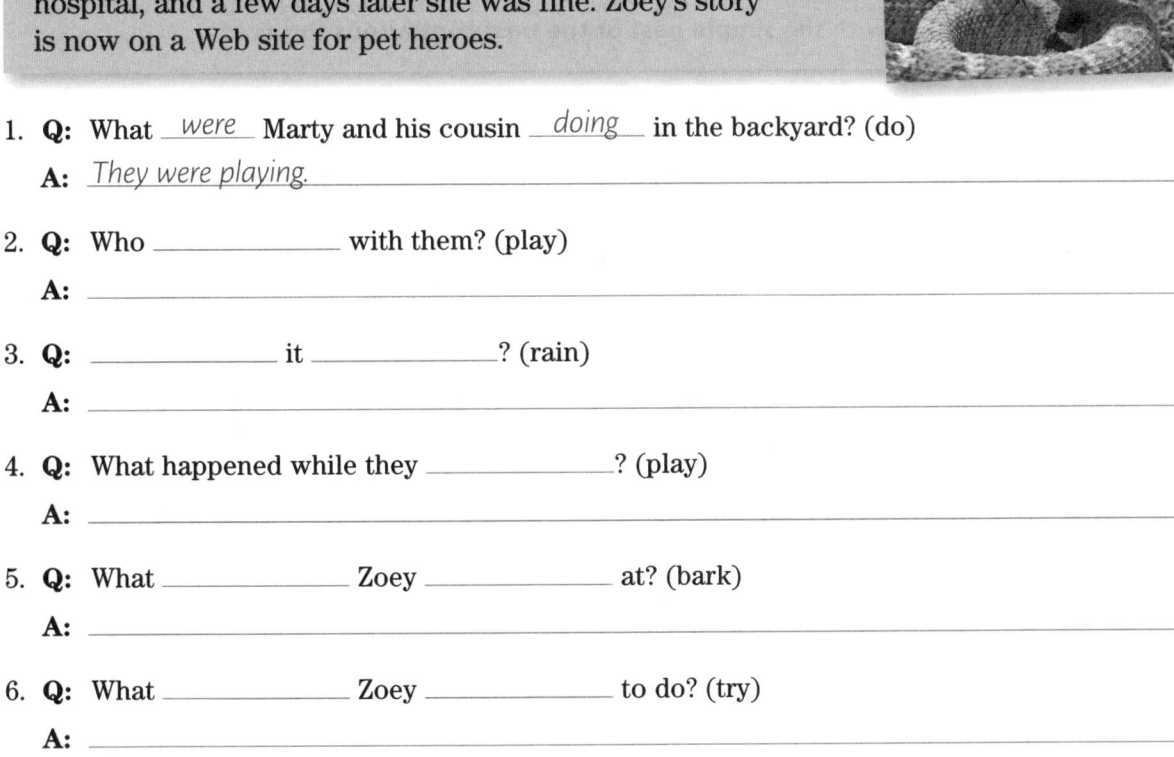

1. Q: What _were_ Marty and his cousin _doing_ in the backyard? (do)
   A: _They were playing._

2. Q: Who _____ with them? (play)
   A: _____

3. Q: _____ it _____? (rain)
   A: _____

4. Q: What happened while they _____? (play)
   A: _____

5. Q: What _____ Zoey _____ at? (bark)
   A: _____

6. Q: What _____ Zoey _____ to do? (try)
   A: _____

Our Stories 47

Lesson 28 — Sharing stories

1 Underline the simple past verb in each sentence. Then circle the past continuous verb in each sentence.

1. My dog saw a squirrel while he was running in the woods.
2. Mrs. Letterman's cell phone rang while she was driving her car.
3. While we were practicing soccer, I hurt my wrist.
4. Hugo ate his dinner while his mother was washing the dishes.
5. We made our campfire while the sun was shining.
6. Jody and Tom got lost while they were riding their bikes in the park.
7. We told scary stories while we were sitting around the campfire.
8. While Allison was chatting online, her brother made dinner.

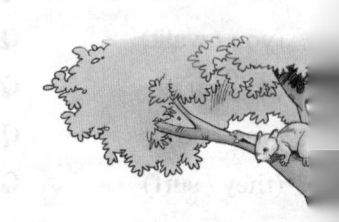

2 Write the simple past and past continuous forms of each verb.

1. fly — _flew_ _was flying_
2. hear ___ ___
3. move ___ ___
4. start ___ ___
5. eat ___ ___
6. touch ___ ___
7. run ___ ___
8. read ___ ___
9. write ___ ___
10. sleep ___ ___
11. call ___ ___
12. laugh ___ ___

3 Complete the story with the simple past or the past continuous forms of the verbs in the box.

☐ do ☐ hear ☐ laugh ☐ make ☐ run ☐ turn on
☐ feel ☐ help ☐ look ☐ (not) see ☐ scream ☑ watch

Anita _was watching_ TV in the living room. It was dark. She _____ a strange noise. Anita _____ around the living room. She _____ anything unusual. Her mother _____ dinner in the kitchen. Her father _____ her mother make dinner. Her brothers _____ homework upstairs. She heard the noise again. This time it was louder. All of a sudden, Anita _____ something on her back. Anita _____! Anita's mother and father _____ into the living room and _____ the light. "What's wrong?" they yelled. Anita turned around and saw her cat, Purrfect. Anita _____ and said she was sorry. Her parents laughed, too.

UNIT 7 Get Connected

1 Read the article quickly. What number did Chuck call?

An Anusual Rescue

We have a new hero right here in Marvindale. Last week, Chuck Edgers was watching the news when he heard a cat meowing loudly. The sound was coming from his neighbor's house. He went to the house, knocked on the front door, but no one answered. The meow got louder. He went to the back of the house. The back door was unlocked, so he pushed it open.

His neighbor, Fred Williams, was sleeping on the couch when Chuck entered the living room. He shook Mr. Williams but he would not wake up. Chuck carried Mr. Williams outside and called 911.

The rescue workers came and helped Mr. Williams. They went into the house and later said his carbon monoxide alarm wasn't working. The cat and Mr. Edgers saved Mr. Williams!

2 Check (✓) the correct answers.

1. **A** I read a great book about Nelson Mandela.
   B ☐ Really? He rescued my cat.   ☑ Really? He's my hero.

2. **A** What's something you need in your house to keep you safe?
   B ☐ A carbon monoxide alarm.   ☐ A cat.

3. **A** My cat was on the roof when I got home from school. It couldn't get down.
   B ☐ Who rescued it?   ☐ Does it meow?

4. **A** How do you open this door?
   B ☐ You enter.   ☐ You push it open.

3 Read the article in Part 1 slowly. Complete the sentences with *before*, *after*, or *when*.

1. Mr. Edgers was watching the news ___when___ he heard a cat meowing.
2. Mr. Edgers went to the front door _____ he went to the back door.
3. Mr. Williams was sleeping _____ Chuck entered his house.
4. Chuck called 911 _____ he was outside.
5. A rescue worker came to the house _____ Chuck called 911.

Our Stories 49

UNIT 7 Check Yourself

1 Match the questions to the answers.

1. Was it windy? _f_
2. What was Sylvia doing? ____
3. Were Mr. and Mrs. Smith watching TV? ____
4. Where was Dan last night? ____
5. What were Brett and Helena doing? ____
6. Was Miranda skiing last weekend? ____

a. He was at the library.
b. They were playing video games.
c. She was buying a new DVD player.
d. Yes, she was.
e. No, they weren't.
f. Yes, it was.

2 Complete the conversation with the sentences in the box.

- ☐ It was raining very hard.
- ☐ I was going to the store.
- ☐ No, she wasn't.
- ☐ Was your sister with you?
- ☐ Well, I was walking along Stewart Street when I saw something weird.
- ☑ What were you doing?
- ☐ Where were you going?
- ☐ You saw a bear when you were walking to the store?

Henry Hey, Ben. I heard you had a scary experience last night. _What were you doing?_
Ben _____
Henry Wow. What did you see?
Ben I'm not sure. _____
Henry That's right. It was very rainy last night. _____
Ben _____ She had a cold, so she stayed home.
Henry _____ Were you going home?
Ben No, I wasn't. _____ I wanted some ice cream. You're going to think I'm crazy, but I think I saw a bear.
Henry _____ You're right! I do think you're crazy!

3 Complete the sentences with both the simple past and the past continuous.

1. do homework
   I _did my homework_ .
   I _was doing my homework_ .

2. not cry
   The baby _____ .
   The baby _____ .

3. shop at the music store
   You _____ .
   You _____ .

4. not watch the movie
   Joan and Alan _____ .
   Joan and Alan _____ .

5. not snow
   It _____ .
   It _____ .

6. use the Internet
   Nicholas _____ .
   Nicholas _____ .

Lesson 29: How do I get there?

1 Complete the conversation with the words in the box.

☐ across ☑ go past ☐ on the corner ☐ turn left
☐ cross ☐ go straight ☐ on your right

Candy Stan, how do I get to your apartment? I'm in front of the subway entrance.

Stan Oh, that's easy. Turn left and _go past_ the bank.

Candy OK.

Stan At the second intersection, _____ the street. Then _____ . There's a nail salon _____ .

Candy Uh-huh. And then?

Stan Then _____ ahead on K Street.

Candy OK. Is your apartment building _____ ?

Stan Yes, it's on the corner. The entrance is _____ from the flower shop.

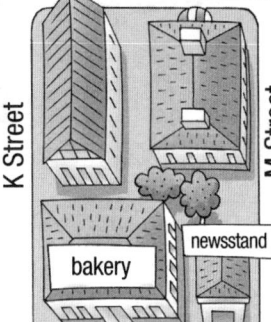

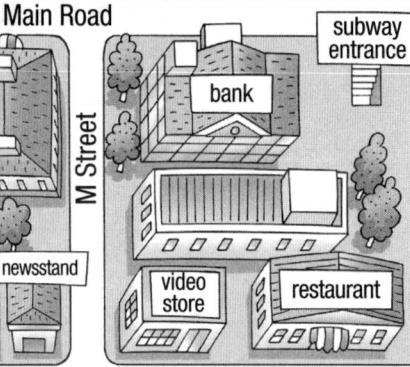

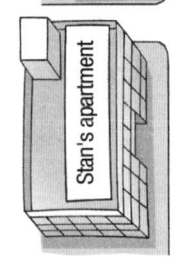

2 Look at the map in Part 1. Then correct the statements.

1. The newsstand is between the bakery and the health club.

   The newsstand is on the corner, next to the bakery.

2. The video store is on the corner, across from the restaurant.

   _____

3. (You're at the grocery store.) Turn right and go straight. Go past the post office. Cross the next intersection. The clothing store is on your left.

   _____

4. (You're at the flower shop.) Turn right and go straight on K Street to the second intersection. Turn left onto Main Road to get to the post office.

   _____

5. (You're at the restaurant.) Turn right and go past the video store, newsstand, and bakery. Turn right onto K Street. Go straight ahead. The nail salon is on the right, on the next corner.

   _____

Lesson 30 · Street fair

1 Alejandro is writing an article for the school newspaper about a street fair. Look at his list of things that were (✔) and weren't (✘) at the street fair. Write sentences with *There was a / some, There were some, There wasn't any,* and *There weren't any.*

Pine Street Fair
✔ good food   ✔ rides
✘ ice cream   ✔ games
✔ a hot-dog stand   ✘ a raffle
✔ a ticket booth   ✘ street vendors

1. There was some good food.
2. _____
3. _____
4. _____
5. _____
6. _____
7. _____
8. _____

2 Write questions with *Was there* and *Were there*. Then write answers.

1. **Q:** (any books for sale) Were there any books for sale?
   A: (yes) Yes, there were.
2. **Q:** (a pizza stand) _____
   A: (no) _____
3. **Q:** (music) _____
   A: (yes) _____
4. **Q:** (flowers for sale) _____
   A: (no) _____

3 Think about a party you attended. Write sentences with positive and negative forms of *There was a* and *There were some*. Use the words in the box and your own information.

☐ cake   ✔ games   ☐ ice cream   ☐ pizza
☐ dancing ☐ gifts   ☐ music   ☐ snacks

1. There weren't any games.
2. _____
3. _____
4. _____
5. _____
6. _____
7. _____
8. _____

Lessons 29 & 30 Mini-review

1 Look at the map. Livvie is new in town. She is in front of her apartment building on Kelly Street. Write answers to her questions.

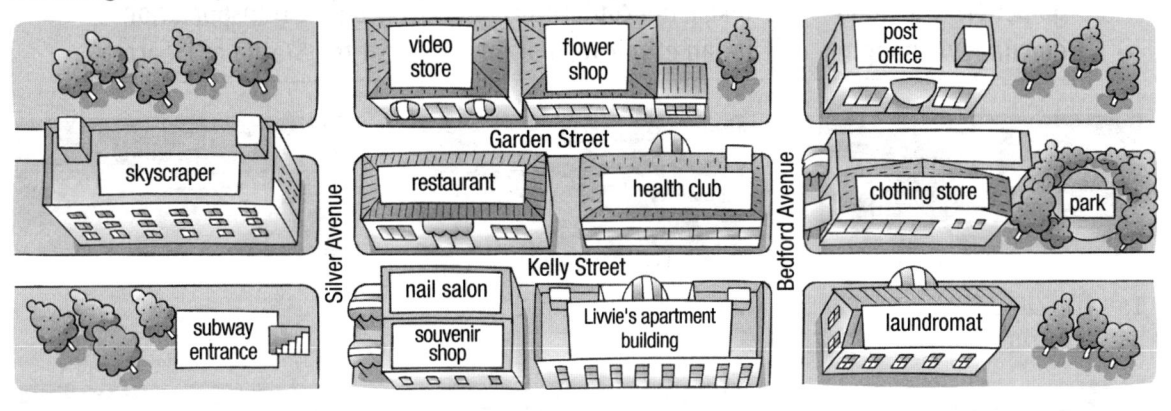

1. **Q:** How do I get to the health club?
   A: *Go to the corner of Bedford Avenue and Kelly Street. Turn left at the intersection. Go straight ahead. Turn left onto Garden Street. The health club is on the left.*

2. **Q:** How do I get to the post office?
   A: _____

3. **Q:** How do I get to the park?
   A: _____

4. **Q:** How do I get to the video store?
   A: _____

2 Trina tells Luis about her vacation. Complete the conversation with *was there, were there, there was, there were,* and the cues.

Luis Hi, Trina. How was your vacation?

Trina Hi, Luis. It was fantastic. I went on a cruise to Mexico.

Luis (any kids your age) *Were there any kids your age?*

Trina (yes) _____ I made some new friends.

Luis (any activities on the cruise) _____

Trina (yes) _____ (a few teen parties) _____

Luis Wow! That sounds great. (a lot of good food) _____

Trina (yes) _____ I ate delicious food every day!

Luis Did you go shopping on the cruise?

Trina No, I didn't. _____ a few stores, but everything was too expensive.

In the City 53

Lesson 31 — Things to do

1 Look at the pictures. Then write suggestions with the words in the box.

- ☐ go people-watching
- ☐ take a helicopter ride
- ☑ try public transportation
- ☐ go window-shopping
- ☐ try an ethnic restaurant
- ☐ visit the Statue of Liberty

1. We could try public transportation.
2. _____
3. _____
4. _____
5. _____
6. _____

2 Write suggestions for 1–4. Write preferences for a–d. Then match the suggestions to the preferences.

1. try an ethnic restaurant

   A We could try an ethnic restaurant.   OR
      Why don't we try an ethnic restaurant?   c

2. take a taxi

   A _____

3. visit a museum

   A _____

4. go to a movie

   A _____

a. go to a concert

   B _____

b. visit a famous landmark

   B _____

c. eat a hamburger

   B I'd rather eat a hamburger.

d. take the bus

   B _____

3 Which would you rather do? Write sentences about your preferences.

1. go skateboarding / go biking I'd rather go skateboarding.
2. sleep late / go to bed early _____
3. clean my room / do homework _____
4. go to a party / go to a movie _____
5. take a boat ride / take a helicopter ride _____
6. eat pizza / try an ethnic restaurant _____

Lesson 32: We didn't go...

1 Rewrite the sentences with the simple past and *because*.

1. Eva goes to Little Italy. She wants Italian food.
   Eva went to Little Italy because she wanted Italian food.

2. Grace doesn't walk to the hotel. She catches the bus.
   _____

3. Will and Carolina don't call their parents. They forget.
   _____

4. Eliza eats in a fast-food restaurant. She wants a hamburger.
   _____

5. Antonio goes to the museum. He wants to see the nature exhibit.
   _____

6. Patricia stays home from school. She isn't feeling well.
   _____

2 Look at the list of things Kelly and Matt did (✓) and didn't (X) do on their family vacation to Colorado. Then write sentences with *because*.

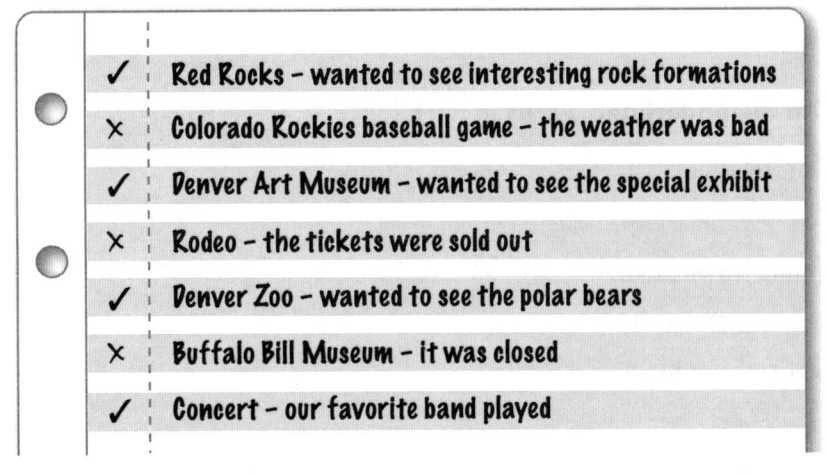

✓	Red Rocks	– wanted to see interesting rock formations
X	Colorado Rockies baseball game	– the weather was bad
✓	Denver Art Museum	– wanted to see the special exhibit
X	Rodeo	– the tickets were sold out
✓	Denver Zoo	– wanted to see the polar bears
X	Buffalo Bill Museum	– it was closed
✓	Concert	– our favorite band played

1. (visit Red Rocks) *We visited Red Rocks because we wanted to see interesting rock formations.*

2. (go to baseball game) _____

3. (visit art museum) _____

4. (go to rodeo) _____

5. (go to zoo) _____

6. (visit museum) _____

7. (go to concert) _____

In the City

UNIT 8 Get Connected

1 Read the Web site quickly. Check (✓) the things you can do in Oahu.

☐ go on the subway   ☐ visit a beach   ☐ visit a harbor

---

www.touristinformationoffice.gc

Welcome to Oahu, Hawaii!

There are many things to do here!

Visit Waikiki Beach. Enjoy the sunshine and swim in Oahu's warm water. It's also a great place to go shopping.

Go to a luau. Eat traditional Hawaiian food and watch traditional Hawaiian dances.

Visit Pearl Harbor. It's a national historic site. See the USS Missouri. It's not a cruise ship. It was a war ship and now it's a museum.

Take a helicopter ride. See Oahu's beaches and rain forest from the sky.

The tourist information office has all the information you need. Visit us every day from 9:00 a.m. – 6:00 p.m.

---

2 Complete the sentences with the underlined words in Part 1.

1. **A** Why don't we fly to Puerto Rico?
   B I'd rather take a _cruise ship_.

2. **A** Let's go window-shopping downtown.
   B I'd rather _____ in the plaza.

3. **A** Is the Alamo in Texas a famous fort?
   B Yes. In fact, it's a _____.

4. We took a _____ because we wanted to have a good view of the harbor.

5. We went to the _____ because the information wasn't online.

3 Read the Web site in Part 1 slowly. Circle the correct words to complete the sentences.

1. This is the (museum's / (tourist information office's)) Web site.
2. You can (take a helicopter ride / go shopping) at Waikiki Beach.
3. You can try Hawaiian food at a (historic site / luau).
4. Go to (Pearl Harbor / Waikiki Beach) to visit a museum.
5. See the rain forest from (the beach / a helicopter).

56 Unit 8

UNIT 8 Check Yourself

1 **Look at the map. Complete the questions with *Was there* and *Were there*. Then answer the questions. Complete the directions with the words in the box.**

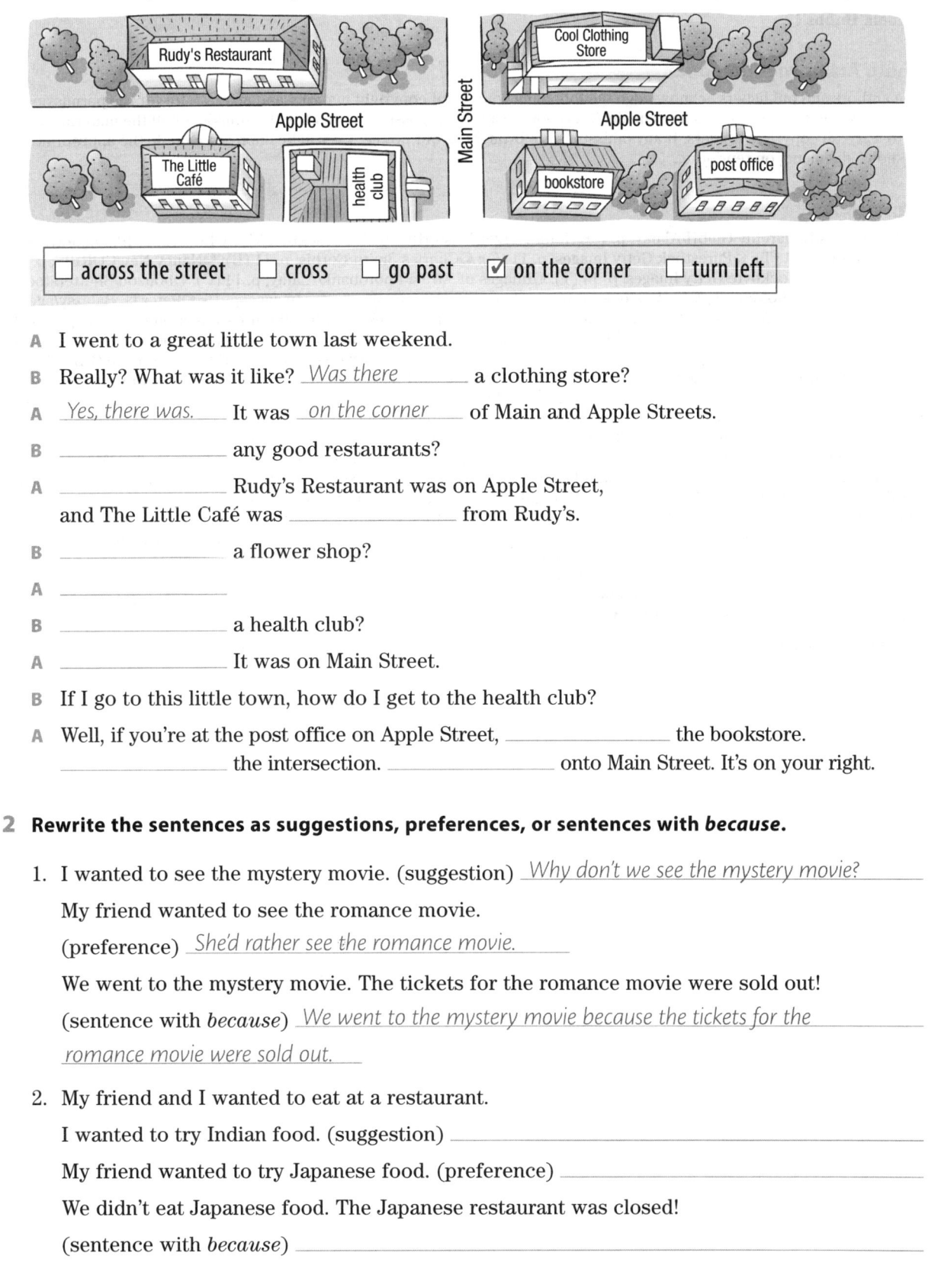

☐ across the street   ☐ cross   ☐ go past   ☑ on the corner   ☐ turn left

A I went to a great little town last weekend.

B Really? What was it like? _Was there_ a clothing store?

A _Yes, there was._ It was _on the corner_ of Main and Apple Streets.

B _____ any good restaurants?

A _____ Rudy's Restaurant was on Apple Street, and The Little Café was _____ from Rudy's.

B _____ a flower shop?

A _____

B _____ a health club?

A _____ It was on Main Street.

B If I go to this little town, how do I get to the health club?

A Well, if you're at the post office on Apple Street, _____ the bookstore. _____ the intersection. _____ onto Main Street. It's on your right.

2 **Rewrite the sentences as suggestions, preferences, or sentences with *because*.**

1. I wanted to see the mystery movie. (suggestion) _Why don't we see the mystery movie?_

   My friend wanted to see the romance movie.
   (preference) _She'd rather see the romance movie._

   We went to the mystery movie. The tickets for the romance movie were sold out!
   (sentence with *because*) _We went to the mystery movie because the tickets for the romance movie were sold out._

2. My friend and I wanted to eat at a restaurant.

   I wanted to try Indian food. (suggestion) _____

   My friend wanted to try Japanese food. (preference) _____

   We didn't eat Japanese food. The Japanese restaurant was closed!
   (sentence with *because*) _____

Illustration Credits

Adolar 6, 24, 41, 51, 53, 57
Chuck Gonzales 8, 12, 18, 31, 39, 44
Marcelo Pacheco 15, 37, 46
Paulo Borges 4, 29, 38, 43, 48
Terry Wong 3, 27, 30, 40, 42
Pamela Hobbs 17

Photo Acknowledgements

The authors and publishers acknowledge the following sources of copyright material and are grateful for the permissions granted. While every effort has been made, it has not always been possible to identify the sources of all the material used, or to trace all copyright holders. If any omissions are brought to our notice, we will be happy to include the appropriate acknowledgements on reprinting.

Workbook

p. 3: ©Juniors Bildarchiv GmbH/Alamy; p. 7: ©Horst Herget/Masterfile; p. 9: ©Stockbyte/Getty Images; p. 10: ©jgorzynik/Shutterstock; p. 11 (T): ©Purestock/Getty Images; p. 11 (C): ©Charles Smith/Corbis; p. 11 (B): ©Nancy Ney/CORBIS; p. 13: ©Comstock/Stockbyte/Getty Images; p. 14 (T): ©Images of Africa Photobank/Alamy; p. 14 (C): ©bouzou/Shutterstock; p. 14 (B): ©Alfie Photography/Shutterstock; p. 15: ©Julian Love/AWL Images/Getty Images; p. 16: ©Peter G. Balazsy/age fotostock/Getty Images; p. 19: ©CORBIS; p. 20: ©Time Life Pictures/NASA/The LIFE Picture Collection/Getty Images; p. 21: ©WorldFoto/Alamy; p. 23: ©Cherryson/Shutterstock; p. 25 (L): ©Xinhua/Alamy; p. 25 (C): ©epa european pressphoto agency b.v./Alamy; p. 25 (R): ©Amy Sussman/Getty Images; p. 26 (T): ©Alexander Hassenstein/Getty Images; p. 26 (CL): ©DEA PICTURE LIBRARY/Getty Images; p. 26 (CR): ©Herschel Hoffmeyer/Shutterstock; p. 26 (BL): ©De Agostini Picture Library/De Agostini/Getty Images; p. 26 (BC): ©Andreas Meyer/Shutterstock; p. 26 (BR): ©Universal Images Group Limited/Alamy; p. 27 (T): ©Maremagnum/Photodisc/Getty Images; p. 27 (B): ©vichie81/Shutterstock; p. 28 (TL): ©Oksana Perkins/iStock/Getty Images Plus/Getty Images; p. 28 (TR): ©Art Kowalsky/Alamy; p. 28 (BL): ©Alistair Baird/Alamy; p. 28 (BR): ©Armin Rose/Shutterstock; p. 32 (T): ©Losevsky Pavel/Shutterstock; p. 32 (B): ©Ruslan Guzov/Shutterstock; p. 33: ©MANDY GODBEHEAR/Shutterstock; p. 34: ©rubberball/Getty Images; p. 35 (T): ©Fuse/Getty Images; p. 35 (B): ©Yadid Levy/Robert Harding World Imagery/Getty Images; p. 36: ©Muriel de Seze/Digital Vision/Getty Images; p. 37: ©Fuse/Getty Images; p. 45 (T): ©BananaStock/Getty Images Plus/Getty Images; p. 45 (B): ©Rich Legg/Stock/Getty Images Plus/Getty Images; p. 47 (T): © RGB Ventures/SuperStock/Alamy; p. 47 (B): ©Rick & Nora Bowers/Alamy; p. 49: ©Georg Bochem/Corbis; p. 54 (TL): ©Kevin Foy/Alamy; p. 54 (TC): ©Image Source/Getty Images; p. 54 (TR): ©Katharina M/Shutterstock; p. 54 (BL): ©Norbert Schaefer/Corbis; p. 54 (BC): ©Mitchell Funk/Photographer's Choice/Getty Images; p. 54 (BR): ©Thinkstock/Stockbyte/Getty Images; p. 55 (T): Picturenet/Blend Images/Getty Images; p. 55 (B): ©Lunnderboy/iStock/Getty Images Plus/Getty Images; p. 56 (L): ©Stock Connection Blue/Alamy; p. 56 (R): ©Ilene MacDonald/Alamy.

Cover photograph by © A. T. Willett/Alamy

Notes

Notes